THE WORLD'S BEST
NOODLES

Norman Kolpas

for Coco ~
my cous cous lover!

In Cannes, Juanles Pinest
now in NYC ~
I ♡ you.
Your Coco

CB
CONTEMPORARY
BOOKS
CHICAGO

Library of Congress Cataloging-in-Publication Data

Kolpas, Norman.
    The world's best noodles / Norman Kolpas.
        p.   cm.
    Includes index.
    ISBN 0-8092-3857-8 (pbk.)
    1. Cookery (Pasta)   2. Cookery, International.   I. Title.
TX809.M17K654   1993
641.8'22—dc20   93-29404
                                                                CIP

Featured on cover: top—Pan-Fried Noodles with Stir-Fried Ginger Chicken and Broccoli (see pg. 31); left—Soba Salad with Smoked Ham and Vegetables (see pg. 80); right—Pad Thai with Shrimp (see pg. 117)

Copyright © 1993 by Norman Kolpas
Published by Contemporary Books, Inc.
Two Prudential Plaza, Chicago, Illinois 60601-6790
Manufactured in the United States of America
International Standard Book Number: 0-8092-3857-8
10   9   8   7   6   5   4   3   2   1

For Katie and Jake

CONTENTS

$\mathcal{A}$CKNOWLEDGMENTS

My thanks to all my friends and relations who happily indulged in noodle testing—and special gratitude to my wife, Katie, and son, Jacob, who are always such cheerful accomplices in the kitchen.

Everyone at Contemporary Books continues to earn my heartfelt appreciation for their support and hard work. Linda Gray in particular deserves thanks for her support of this book, and for always being such a helpful, understanding, and good-humored editor.

$\mathcal{I}$NTRODUCTION

Not so very long ago, we viewed the world of noodles from a very limited perspective. First and foremost was the pasta of Italy, in all its glorious variety. Second, of significantly lesser culinary importance, were the various egg noodles found elsewhere in Europe and America, and the occasional seemingly adventurous journey into Cantonese *chow mein*. And that was it.

With the culinary revolution of the past decades, we've happily come to realize how limited this Western view of noodles really was. As our tastes grew broader, embracing the cuisines of Thailand, Japan, Korea, Indonesia, Vietnam, the Philippines—not to mention the many regional variations of Chinese cooking—one of the things we came to realize was just how varied noodles really can be. There are wondrously flavorful noodles made from rice and from buckwheat. Noodles also are made from vegetable starches, with an almost ethereal translucency. Wonderful Chinese noodles that are a world away from the crisp-fried canned *chow mein* fare we all munched on during the 1950s and 1960s also are available.

As far as we've come in our appreciation of the world's noodles, however, I don't think we've yet come far enough. Sure, we may eat them in our favorite ethnic restaurants—but most of us have not yet discovered the joy of cooking international noodle dishes in our own kitchens.

This book's goal is to pave the way for you to do just that: to familiarize yourself with the world's noodles and start savoring them at home. In doing so, this cookbook doesn't limit itself merely to the noodles of Asia. It also includes a generous helping of traditional egg-noodle dishes from Europe and America, as well as recipes for a little-known cousin of noodles and pasta: the couscous of North Africa.

Because unfamiliar foreign terminology, ingredients, and techniques often can frustrate the home cook, the recipes in this book strive above all for simplicity. Each chapter begins with a brief, straightforward discussion of the kind of noodle or noodles used in its recipes and the basic ways in which they are prepared; there's no need to flip elsewhere in the book for information you might need. Likewise, special ingredients are briefly defined in the introductory notes and shopping lists for each recipe in which they appear; again, you won't have to flip through the book to look up their definitions in a separate glossary.

After you've tried a few recipes, you'll begin to see that preparing these wonderful dishes is as easy as—or even easier than—any pasta recipes you might have in your everyday repertoire. Please feel free to add your favorites among these recipes to your own personal files, changing or elaborating on them as familiarity grows and inspiration strikes you.

A BRIEF NOTE ON BUYING
AND SUBSTITUTING NOODLES

❧

Once you start looking for them, you'll no doubt be surprised by how widely available the noodles called for in this book really are. Most good-sized towns today have Asian markets. Just stroll down their aisles and you're likely to find some dried form of egg, wheat, rice, buckwheat, and bean-thread noodles; the refrigerator or freezer cases may well offer you the further option of freshly made noodles.

What's more, the widespread interest in the world's cuisines has led well-stocked supermarkets and specialty foods stores to carry a wider array of international ingredients—including many of the kinds of noodles mentioned here. Seek out the best such markets in your area and take a close look in their foreign-foods aisles. If you can't find what you're looking for, ask the manager to order it for you.

But, most important, don't be discouraged from making these recipes if you can't find the specific noodles called for. Just substitute a pasta or noodle of similar size and shape, regardless of what it is made from. Fresh or dried Italian linguine or fettucine, for example, can be used in place of ribbon-shaped Asian egg, wheat, or even rice noodles.

Fine Italian vermicelli, cappellini, cappelletti, or angel hair can be substituted, if necessary, for fine bean threads, rice noodles, or *chow mein*. Even buckwheat noodles have a Western substitute, for most health-food stores carry some form of spaghetti or other pasta strands made from buckwheat flour.

BASIC PREPARATIONS

ROASTED PEPPERS

Oven-roasted peppers bring intense color, tender texture, and rich flavor to noodle dishes.

To roast peppers, place them on a baking sheet in the middle of a 500°F oven. Roast until their skins are evenly blistered and browned, about 25 minutes, turning them two or three times so they roast evenly. Remove them from the oven and cover with a kitchen towel.

When the peppers are cool enough to handle, pull out the stems, peel away the blackened skins, open the peppers up, and remove the seeds, using a teaspoon to pick up any strays. Then tear or cut the roasted peppers as directed in the recipe.

A NOTE ON CHILI PEPPERS

Some recipes in this book call for fresh or roasted chili peppers, which contain oils that can cause a painful burning sensation on contact with the eyes or the skin. To prevent this from happening, take special care when handling chilies:

Use kitchen gloves if necessary, particularly if you have any cuts or abrasions or if your skin tends to be sensitive.

After handling chilies, wash your hands liberally with plenty of warm, soapy water.

Be very careful not to touch your eyes after handling chilies. If you do so accidentally, splash plenty of cool water in your eyes to rinse them.

TOASTED NUTS

Nuts add rich flavor and crisp texture to noodle dishes.

To toast nuts, start with plain shelled or blanched nutmeats that have not been roasted, salted, or otherwise cooked or seasoned.

Preheat the oven to 325°F. Spread the nuts in a single layer on a baking sheet and bake just until light golden brown: 1 to 2 minutes for sesame seeds, no more than 3 to 5 minutes or so for small nuts such as pine nuts or slivered almonds, and up to 10 minutes for larger, whole nuts. Be sure to check frequently to prevent the nuts from burning; they will continue to darken slightly after you remove them from the oven.

Once cooled, store toasted nuts in an airtight container to safeguard their crispness.

SOME ADVICE ON SERVING
AND EATING NOODLE DISHES

❧

Particularly with Asian noodles, your presentation of the finished recipe can gain added beauty and interest if you use traditional serving dishes. In most ethnic stores where you might buy your noodles, you're likely to find surprisingly inexpensive tableware—bowls, platters, dishes, and so on. By the same token, when serving Asian dishes, you also may wish to offer your family or friends chopsticks—and, when serving soups, the gracefully shaped and decorated ceramic or plastic spoons one often sees in Chinese or Japanese restaurants.

These little touches can help turn your meal into a more festive occasion—but they're certainly not required! Above all, make sure that you and your guests feel comfortable with the food that you serve. Any of the recipes in this book will look fine on simple serving pieces, whatever their origin. And if a fork will convey noodles from dish to mouth with less embarrassment than chopsticks, by all means make a fork available to whomever might wish to use it.

A NOTE ON SERVING QUANTITIES

❧

All of the recipes in this book are intended to yield four generous servings as a featured dish; the recipes are easily doubled or tripled. If serving them as one of several dishes in a larger meal or a buffet, they will correspondingly serve more people—generally six to eight side-dish servings from a single recipe.

1
ASIAN EGG AND WHEAT NOODLES

Dan-meen. Mee. Ba-mee. These, and many other names, refer to Asian *egg* noodles.

Lo mein. Chow mein. Somen. Udon. Ramen. These, and other names, refer to the main *wheat* noodles of Asia.

Traditional recipes utilizing either of these noodle categories alone could fill an entire book—or more. For the scope of this volume, however, they are grouped together for the simple reason that such noodles often are interchangeable.

Go to any Asian market and you'll find them fresh in the refrigerated case, fresh-frozen in the freezer section, and dried on the open shelves. You'll see varying shapes and sizes called by the same name, and similar noodles called by different names. You'll even find "egg-flavored noodles"—a hybrid that, with its yellow hue, looks like egg noodles but contains little if any egg. Consult an Asian cookbook or two and you'll find similar recipes calling for different kinds of noodles.

The recipes that follow take note of such confusion—along with the fact that, in any given city or town, only a limited number of options are likely to be available. For the most part, these recipes suggest a specific kind of noodle—the most authentic to the dish's country of origin—but then go on to offer more general options. In a pinch, you can even use fine European egg noodles or pasta.

Whatever kind of noodle or pasta you use, take care to follow the cooking instructions on the package and pay attention during boiling to ensure that the noodles do not overcook—particularly when using fresh or frozen egg noodles, which require no more than a few minutes of boiling.

Noodle Soup with Chicken Broth and Spinach

CHINA

This is a simple, satisfying version of lunchtime soup noodles.

> 2 quarts chicken broth
> 1 pound fresh or ¾ pound dried thin to
>   medium Asian egg or wheat noodles
> 1½ cups packed fresh spinach leaves,
>   thoroughly washed, trimmed, and cut
>   crosswise into ¼- to ½-inch-wide shreds
> ¼ cup light soy sauce
> ¼ cup thinly sliced fresh scallions

Put the broth in a large saucepan and bring to a boil over high heat. Reduce the heat to very low, cover, and reserve.

Bring a separate pan of water to a boil and cook the noodles until tender. Drain the noodles, rinse briefly under cold running water, drain again, and toss gently with the spinach shreds. Divide the noodle-spinach mixture among four large serving bowls, mounding the mixture in the center. Stir the soy sauce into the reserved broth and ladle the broth into the bowls. Garnish with scallions.

MAKES 4 SERVINGS

Noodle Soup with Egg and Seaweed

JAPAN

Dried sheets of seaweed, known as *nori,* are widely available in Japanese markets. The heat of the broth, ladled over them at serving time, instantly softens the strips of *nori* to tenderness.

1½ quarts chicken broth
1 quart beef broth
1 pound fresh or ¾ pound dried thin to
*   medium Asian egg or wheat noodles*
4 square sheets nori, *stacked and cut*
*   with a large sharp knife into ¼-inch-*
*   wide strips*
¼ cup light soy sauce
2 eggs, hard-boiled, peeled, and cut into
*   halves*
¼ cup thinly sliced fresh scallions

Put the broths in a large saucepan and bring to a boil over high heat. Reduce the heat to very low, cover, and reserve.

Bring a separate pan of water to a boil and cook the noodles until tender.

Drain the noodles and divide them among four large serving bowls, mounding the noodles in the center. Scatter the *nori* strips over the noodles. Stir the soy sauce into the reserved broth and ladle the broth into the bowls. Top each mound of noodles with half of an egg and garnish with scallions.

MAKES 4 SERVINGS

Clear Soup with Ramen, Stir-Fried Vegetables, and Kimchee

JAPAN

❧

Though the topping of this main-course soup is fairly light, it gains breathtaking flavor and color from the addition of fresh, chili-spiced Korean pickled cabbage—kimchee—available bottled or canned in Asian markets. The clear broth provides a light, refreshing contrast to the other colorful ingredients.

—8—

1½ quarts beef broth
1 quart chicken broth
1 pound fresh or ¾ pound dried ramen or other thin Asian wheat or egg noodles
2 tablespoons vegetable oil
2 medium-sized leaves bok choy or Nappa cabbage, trimmed and cut crosswise into ¼-inch-wide slices
1 medium-sized carrot, cut into ¼-inch-thick diagonal slices

1 medium-sized green bell pepper, quartered, stemmed, seeded, and cut crosswise into ¼-inch-wide slices
¼ pound fresh mushrooms, cut into ¼-inch-thick slices
½ cup drained canned sliced water chestnuts
1 to 1½ cups kimchee
½ cup thinly sliced fresh scallions

Put the broths in a large saucepan and bring to a boil over high heat. Reduce the heat to very low, cover, and reserve.

Bring a separate pan of water to a boil and cook the *ramen* until tender. Drain well.

Meanwhile, in a wok or large skillet, heat the oil over moderately high heat. Add the bok choy, carrot, bell pepper, mushrooms, and water chestnuts; stir-fry just until the vegetables are tender-crisp, 2 to 3 minutes.

Divide the *ramen* among four large serving bowls, mounding the noodles in the center. Ladle the reserved broth into the bowls. Spoon the stir-fried vegetable mixture on top of the noodles. Decoratively drape the pieces of kimchee over and around the vegetables. Garnish with scallions.

MAKES 4 SERVINGS

Noodle Soup with Stir-Fried Pork and Pickled Vegetables

CHINA

Szechuan-style preserved vegetables, available in Asian markets add a bracing tang to the stir-fried pork topping in this popular Chinese main-course noodle soup.

2 tablespoons light soy sauce
1 teaspoon cornstarch
½ pound boneless pork fillet, well trimmed
   and cut into 2-inch by ¼-inch strips
2 quarts chicken broth
1 pound fresh or ¾ pound dried thin to
   medium Asian egg or wheat noodles
2 tablespoons vegetable oil
½ cup bottled or canned Szechuan
   preserved vegetables
½ cup thinly sliced fresh scallions

In a mixing bowl, stir together 1 tablespoon of the soy sauce with the cornstarch. Add the pork and toss well. Cover and refrigerate about 30 minutes.

Put the broth in a large saucepan and bring to a boil over high heat. Reduce the heat to very low, cover, and reserve.

Bring a separate pan of water to a boil. Cook the noodles until tender. Drain well.

Meanwhile, in a wok or large skillet, heat the oil over moderately high heat. Add the pork and stir-fry until it loses its pink color, 1 to 2 minutes. Add the preserved vegetables and stir-fry 1 to 2 minutes more.

Divide the noodles among four large serving bowls, mounding the noodles in the center. Stir the remaining soy sauce into the reserved broth and ladle the broth into the bowls. Spoon the stir-fried pork-and-vegetable mixture on top of the noodles and garnish with scallions.

MAKES 4 SERVINGS

Soy Soup with Ramen, Seafood, and Vegetables

JAPAN

❧

A splash of light soy sauce adds extra flavor to this main-course soup. The squid adds extra interest with its chewy texture and mild, sweet flavor; but feel free to leave it out or otherwise vary the assortment or proportions of seafood. Dried *shiitake* mushrooms, available in Asian markets or supermarket specialty food sections, contribute their own meaty taste and texture.

1½ quarts beef broth

1 quart chicken broth

1 pound fresh or ¾ pound dried ramen or other thin Asian wheat or egg noodles

3 tablespoons vegetable oil

¼ pound small to medium-sized fresh shrimp, shelled and deveined

¼ pound fresh bay scallops, trimmed

2 baby squid, cleaned, bodies cut into ¼-inch rings, tentacles cut into small clusters

4 dried shiitake mushrooms, soaked in warm water until soft, rinsed well, stems trimmed off and discarded, caps cut into ¼-inch-wide pieces

2 medium-sized leaves bok choy or Nappa cabbage, trimmed and cut crosswise into ¼-inch-wide slices

1 medium-sized carrot, cut into ¼-inch-thick diagonal slices

1 medium-sized green bell pepper, quartered, stemmed, seeded, and cut crosswise into ¼-inch-wide slices

Salt and white pepper

¼ cup light soy sauce

½ cup thinly sliced fresh scallions

Put the broths in a large saucepan and bring to a boil over high heat. Reduce the heat to very low, cover, and reserve.

Bring a separate pan of water to a boil and cook the *ramen* until tender. Drain well.

Meanwhile, in a wok or large skillet, heat half of the oil over moderately high heat. Add the shrimp, scallops, and squid and stir-fry until the shrimp turn pink, 1 to 2 minutes; remove and set aside. Heat the remaining oil in the wok and add the *shiitake* mushrooms, bok choy, carrot, and bell pepper; stir-fry just until the vegetables are tender-crisp, 2 to 3 minutes. Return the reserved seafood to the wok, season to taste with salt and white pepper, and stir briefly to mix.

Divide the *ramen* among four large serving bowls, mounding the noodles in the center. Stir the soy sauce into the reserved broth and ladle the broth into the bowls. Spoon the stir-fried seafood-and-vegetable mixture on top of the noodles. Garnish with scallions.

MAKES 4 SERVINGS

Soy Soup with Ramen and Crab Egg Foo Young

JAPAN

A generous slice of flat crab-and-egg omelet tops each portion of noodles in this version of the popular main-course noodle soup. Substitute cooked bay shrimp for the crab. Dried *shiitake* mushrooms, found in Asian markets and supermarket specialty food aisles, enrich the omelet's taste and texture.

> 2½ quarts chicken broth
> 1 pound fresh or ¾ pound dried ramen
>   or other thin Asian wheat or egg
>   noodles
> ¼ cup vegetable oil
> 2 medium-sized scallions, sliced thin
> 1 tablespoon grated fresh gingerroot
> 4 dried shiitake mushrooms, soaked in
>   warm water until soft, rinsed well,
>   stems trimmed off and discarded, caps
>   cut into ¼-inch-wide pieces
> ½ pound flaked cooked crabmeat
> 6 tablespoons light soy sauce
> 6 eggs, well beaten
> Salt and white pepper
> 2 tablespoons finely chopped fresh
>   cilantro

Put the broth in a large saucepan and bring to a boil over high heat. Reduce the heat to very low, cover, and reserve.

Bring a separate pan of water to a boil and cook the *ramen* until tender. Drain well.

Meanwhile, in a heavy, medium-sized nonstick skillet, heat half of the oil over moderately high heat. Add the scallions and ginger and stir-fry 1 minute. Add the *shiitake* mushrooms, crab, and 2 tablespoons of the soy sauce and stir-fry 1 minute more.

Transfer the crab mixture to a bowl, stir in the eggs, and season to taste with salt and white pepper. Heat the remaining oil in the skillet over moderate heat and spread the crab-and-egg mixture evenly in the skillet. As soon as the underside is set and light golden, about 2 minutes, loosen the edges, shake the skillet to make sure the pancake isn't sticking, and cover with the skillet lid or a large plate; carefully invert the lid and skillet together, then slide the pancake back into the skillet and cook 1 to 2 minutes more.

Divide the *ramen* among four large serving bowls, mounding the noodles in the center. Stir the remaining soy sauce into the reserved broth and ladle the broth into the bowls. Slide the egg foo young onto a cutting board and cut into four equal wedges. With a spatula, pick up each wedge and drape it over the noodles in a bowl. Garnish with cilantro.

MAKES 4 SERVINGS

Miso Soup with Ramen and Stir-Fried Pork and Vegetables

JAPAN

Soup with noodles is a favorite midday meal throughout Japan. Feel free to substitute beef or chicken for the pork. *Mirin*, a syrupy Japanese cooking wine available in Asian and many Western markets, enhances the pork's natural sweetness. Miso, the widely available pasta of fermented soybeans, enriches the broth.

½ pound boneless pork fillet, well trimmed and sliced thin

2 tablespoons light soy sauce

1 tablespoon mirin (Japanese sweet rice wine)

1½ quarts beef broth

1 quart chicken broth

1 pound fresh or ¾ pound dried ramen or other thin Asian wheat or egg noodles

2 tablespoons vegetable oil

1 medium-sized carrot, cut into ¼-inch-thick diagonal slices

1 medium-sized celery stalk, cut into ¼-inch-thick diagonal slices

1 medium-sized green bell pepper, quartered, stemmed, seeded, and cut crosswise into ¼-inch-wide slices

1 cup bean sprouts

¼ cup Japanese red miso

½ cup thinly sliced fresh scallions

In a mixing bowl, toss the pork slices with the soy sauce and *mirin*. Cover and marinate about 15 minutes.

Put the broths in a large saucepan and bring to a boil over high heat. Reduce the heat to very low, cover, and reserve.

Bring a separate pan of water to a boil and cook the *ramen* until tender. Drain well.

Meanwhile, in a wok or large skillet, heat the oil over moderately high heat. Drain the pork and add it, stir-frying until it loses its pink color, 1 to 2 minutes. Add the carrot, celery, bell pepper, and bean sprouts and stir-fry just until the vegetables are tender-crisp, 2 to 3 minutes.

Divide the *ramen* among four large serving bowls, mounding the noodles in the center. Stir the miso into the reserved broth until it dissolves completely, and ladle the broth into the bowls. Spoon the stir-fried pork-and-vegetable mixture on top of the noodles and garnish with scallions.

MAKES 4 SERVINGS

Mabo Soup with Udon, Minced Pork, and Tofu

JAPAN

A rich, savory, slightly spicy mixture of pork and tofu, enriched with miso—fermented soybean paste—and the chopped caps of chewy *shiitake* mushrooms, tops coarse Japanese wheat noodles in this main-course soup. Try it with ground chicken instead of pork, if you like. Asian egg noodles can, of course, be substituted for the *udon*.

1½ quarts beef broth
1 quart chicken broth
1 pound fresh or ¾ pound dried udon *or other thick Asian wheat or egg noodles*
2 tablespoons vegetable oil
2 medium-sized garlic cloves, chopped fine
1 tablespoon grated fresh gingerroot
½ pound ground pork
4 dried shiitake *mushrooms, soaked in warm water until soft, rinsed well, stems trimmed off and discarded, caps coarsely chopped*
½ pound firm Chinese-style tofu, drained and cut into ½-inch cubes
1 medium-sized carrot, shredded
¼ cup Japanese red miso
2 tablespoons hot chili oil
2 tablespoons rice vinegar
1 tablespoon light soy sauce
Salt and white pepper
½ cup thinly sliced fresh scallions

Put the broths in a large saucepan and bring to a boil over high heat. Reduce the heat to very low, cover, and reserve.

Bring a separate pan of water to a boil and cook the *udon* until tender. Drain well.

Meanwhile, in a wok or large skillet, heat the oil over moderately high heat. Add the garlic and ginger and stir-fry for 1 minute. Add the pork and *shiitake* mushrooms and stir-fry, breaking up the pork, until the pork just begins to brown, 4 to 5 minutes.

Add the tofu, carrot, miso, ¼ cup of the reserved warm broth, the chili oil, rice vinegar, and soy sauce. Simmer, stirring, until the mixture is thick and uniformly heated, 2 to 3 minutes. Season to taste with salt and white pepper. Stir in the scallions.

Divide the *udon* among four large serving bowls, mounding the noodles in the center. Ladle the remaining broth into the bowls. Spoon the pork-and-tofu mixture on top of the noodles.

—17—

MAKES 4 SERVINGS

Spicy Coconut Soup with Shrimp and Noodles

INDONESIA

Coconut milk, which is available in Asian markets and specialty food shops, mediates the spiciness of this main-course noodle soup. The lemongrass and bottled fish sauce respectively contribute a refreshing tang and a rich, bracing saltiness to the soup.

*¾ pound fresh or ½ pound dried thin
   Asian egg or wheat noodles
1½ quarts chicken broth
2 (¼-inch-thick) slices fresh gingerroot
2 stalks fresh lemongrass, cut into 2-inch
   pieces, or 2 long strips lemon zest
¾ pound fresh small to medium-sized
   shrimp, shelled and deveined
1 cup canned or bottled coconut milk
2 tablespoons fish sauce
2 tablespoons hot chili oil
1 cup bean sprouts
2 medium-sized scallions, sliced thin
¼ cup coarsely chopped fresh cilantro
1 lime, cut into wedges*

Bring a large pan of water to a boil, add the noodles, and cook until tender. At the same time, put the broth, ginger, and lemongrass in another pan and bring to a boil over moderate heat. Reduce the heat, cover, and simmer 3 minutes; add the shrimp and simmer until done, about 2 minutes. Remove the shrimp from the pan and set aside; stir in the coconut milk, fish sauce, and chili oil and bring the liquid back to a simmer.

Drain the noodles and mound them in four individual serving bowls. Arrange the reserved shrimp on top and ladle the hot soup into each bowl. Garnish with bean sprouts, scallions, and cilantro. Serve with lime wedges for each guest to squeeze in to taste.

MAKES 4 SERVINGS

Somen Salad with Chicken, Egg, Vegetables, and Soy-Ginger Dressing

Cool, clean-tasting, and refreshing, this easy noodle dish makes an ideal light warm-weather lunch. The dashi is a light Japanese dried bonito broth brewed from small pouches resembling tea bags. It is available in Japanese markets. The red pickled ginger—the kind served as a sweet-hot garnish in sushi restaurants—is also available in Japanese markets.

¾ cup light soy sauce
¾ cup rice vinegar
½ cup brewed dashi
2 tablespoons sugar
1 tablespoon dry sherry
2 teaspoons grated fresh gingerroot
1 pound dried somen or other fine Asian wheat noodles
1½ cups finely shredded cooked chicken breast

2 hard-boiled eggs, sliced thin
1 small red bell pepper, quartered, stemmed, seeded, quarters cut crosswise into thin slices
½ cup shredded daikon (Japanese white radish)
½ cup daikon sprouts
¼ cup Japanese sliced red pickled ginger, cut into thin shreds

—19—

In a mixing bowl, stir together the soy sauce, vinegar, dashi, sugar, sherry, and ginger. Cover and refrigerate until well chilled.

Bring a large pan of water to a boil, add the *somen*, and cook until tender. Drain and rinse under cold running water until the noodles are cool. Drain well.

Divide the noodles among four individual serving bowls, mounding the noodles in the center. Arrange the remaining ingredients decoratively on top. Pour the soy-ginger mixture around the sides of the noodles to half-submerge them.

MAKES 4 SERVINGS

Dan Dan Mein Salad with Chicken and Cucumber

CHINA

This is a variation on the basic *dan dan* noodle dish, a specialty of Chinese street vendors. Here it is transformed into a luscious cool-and-spicy main-course salad. Be sure to use Asian sesame oil, available in Asian markets and well-stocked food stores; made from toasted seeds, it has a richer color and flavor than conventional cold-pressed sesame oil.

4 large garlic cloves
½ cup light soy sauce
¼ cup brown sugar
½ cup unsalted peanut butter
2 tablespoons sesame paste
½ cup chicken broth
1½ tablespoons hot chili oil
¾ pound fresh or ½ pound dried thin
  Asian egg or wheat noodles
1 tablespoon Asian sesame oil
1 large cucumber, peeled, halved
  lengthwise, seeded, and cut into long,
  thin shreds
1½ cups coarsely chopped cooked chicken
2 medium-sized scallions, sliced thin
⅓ cup coarsely chopped toasted peanuts
  (see Index)
1 tablespoon finely chopped fresh
  cilantro

Put the garlic in a food processor and pulse the machine, stopping to scrape down the bowl, until chopped fine. Stir together the soy sauce and sugar until the sugar dissolves, then add them to the processor bowl with the peanut butter, sesame paste, broth, and chili oil. Pulse several times, then process until smoothly blended. Set aside.

Bring a large pan of water to a boil, add the noodles, and cook until tender.

When the noodles are done, drain well, add to a mixing bowl, and toss with the sesame oil until evenly coated. Let cool to room temperature.

Transfer the noodles to one large or four individual serving bowls. Ladle the sauce generously on top. Arrange a ring of cucumber around the sides of each bowl and scatter the chicken pieces in the center. Garnish with scallions, peanuts, and cilantro.

MAKES 4 SERVINGS

Somen Salad with Shredded Vegetables and Miso Mayonnaise

JAPAN

❧

Although many tend to think of mayonnaise as a dressing of the Western world, the Japanese are quite fond of it. Here, the creamy sauce, combined with miso—soybean paste—makes a luxurious dressing for a colorful, fresh mixture of simple wheat noodles and vegetables, including dark, chewy strips of *shiitake* mushroom and shreds of sweet-hot pickled ginger.

¾ cup mayonnaise

3 tablespoons Japanese yellow miso

1 tablespoon dry sherry

2 teaspoons sugar

1 pound dried somen *or other fine Asian wheat noodles*

¼ pound snow peas, blanched in boiling water for 30 seconds, drained, and cut diagonally into thin strips

8 dried shiitake *mushrooms, soaked in warm water until soft, rinsed well, stems trimmed off and discarded, caps cut into thin slices*

2 medium-sized scallions, cut into 1-inch shreds

1 small red bell pepper, quartered, stemmed, seeded, quarters cut crosswise into thin slices

¼ cup Japanese sliced red pickled ginger, cut into thin shreds

1 tablespoon black sesame seeds

In a mixing bowl, stir together the mayonnaise, miso, sherry, and sugar. Cover and refrigerate.

Bring a large pan of water to a boil, add the *somen*, and cook until tender. Drain and rinse under cold running water until the noodles are cool. Drain well.

In a mixing bowl, gently toss together the noodles, snow peas, mushrooms, scallions, bell pepper, and ginger with enough dressing to coat them. Garnish with sesame seeds.

MAKES 4 SERVINGS

Dan Dan Mein

CHINA

You'll find this popular Chinese street vendor's specialty also transliterated as *tan tan, don don*, and many other spellings—all attempting to capture the sound made by the vendor's clapper to herald his or her arrival. There are just as many versions of the dish as there are spellings, each combining long egg noodles with a smooth, spicy sauce enriched with peanut butter and Asian-style sesame oil made from toasted sesame seeds.

4 large garlic cloves
½ cup light soy sauce
¼ cup brown sugar
⅔ cup unsalted peanut butter
½ cup chicken broth
1½ tablespoons hot chili oil
1 tablespoon Asian sesame oil
¾ pound fresh or ½ pound dried thin
   Asian egg or wheat noodles
2 tablespoons peanut oil
2 medium-sized scallions, sliced thin
1 tablespoon finely chopped fresh cilantro

Put the garlic in a food processor and pulse the machine, stopping to scrape down the bowl, until chopped fine. Stir together the soy sauce and sugar until the sugar dissolves, then add them to the processor bowl with the peanut butter, broth, and chili and sesame oils. Pulse several times, then process until smoothly blended. Set aside.

Bring a large pan of water to a boil, add the noodles, and cook until tender.

Heat the peanut oil in a wok or skillet over moderate heat. Add the reserved peanut-butter mixture and cook, stirring, just until warmed through, 2 to 3 minutes.

When the noodles are done, drain well. Transfer to one large or four individual serving bowls, ladle the sauce generously on top, and garnish with scallions and cilantro.

MAKES 4 SERVINGS

Pan-Fried Noodles with Monk's Vegetables and Tofu

CHINA

This traditional vegetable dish proves that a Buddhist monk's strict diet need not require total self-denial. Feel free to vary the mixture of vegetables with your own favorites or whatever is at the peak of season; but try to include *shiitake* mushrooms, available in Asian markets and well-stocked supermarkets, for their meaty flavor and texture. Use vegetable broth if you want a strictly vegetarian meal, chicken broth if you plan to serve the dish alongside meat or poultry. Use a metal serving spoon, or a knife if necessary, to cut through the crisply browned noodle pancake before serving it with the stir-fried mixture.

¾ *pound fresh or* ½ *pound dried thin Asian egg or wheat noodles*

1½ *cups peanut or corn oil*

3 *medium-sized garlic cloves, chopped fine*

2 *medium-sized carrots, cut diagonally into* ¼*-inch-thick slices*

1 *medium-sized onion, chopped coarse*

1 *medium-sized red or green bell pepper, quartered, stemmed, seeded, quarters cut crosswise into* ¼*-inch-wide slices*

4 *medium-sized leaves Nappa cabbage, cut crosswise into* ¼*-inch-wide slices*

¼ *pound small snow peas, trimmed*

8 *dried* shiitake *mushrooms, soaked in warm water until soft, rinsed well, stems trimmed off and discarded, caps cut into* ¼*-inch-wide slices*

½ *cup drained canned whole baby corn*

1¼ *cups vegetable or chicken broth*

¼ *cup light soy sauce*

1½ *tablespoons cornstarch*

½ *pound firm Chinese-style tofu, drained well on paper towels and cut into* ½*-inch cubes*

Salt and white pepper

¼ *cup slivered almonds, toasted (see Index)*

Bring a large pan of water to a boil, add the noodles, and cook until tender. Drain, rinse under cold running water, and drain well again.

In a heavy medium-sized skillet, heat 1¼ cups of the oil over moderate heat. Add the drained noodles, using a wooden spatula or spoon to spread them evenly and press them gently, forming an even, loose cake. Fry until their underside is golden brown, 5 to 7 minutes, checking frequently to avoid burning. Then carefully turn the cake over to cook the other side.

A minute or two before turning the noodles, heat the remaining oil in a large wok or skillet over high heat. Add the garlic; as soon as it sizzles, add the carrots, onion, and bell pepper, stir-frying 2 to 3 minutes. Add the cabbage, snow peas, mushrooms, and baby corn and stir-fry 1 minute more. Add the broth, stirring and scraping to deglaze. Stir together the soy sauce and cornstarch; as soon as the liquid in the wok simmers, stir in the soy mixture and add the tofu. Continue simmering, gently stirring to mix in the tofu without breaking it up, until the tofu is heated through and the liquid thickens to coat all the ingredients, 2 to 3 minutes. Taste the sauce and adjust the seasoning with salt and white pepper.

While the liquid simmers, remove the browned noodles from the skillet and drain on paper towels. Transfer to a heated platter and mound the vegetable mixture on top of the noodles. Garnish with almonds.

MAKES 4 SERVINGS

Pan-Fried Noodles with Sweet and Sour Stir-Fried Shrimp

CHINA

This version of sweet and sour forgoes the familiar deep-fried batter coating—an improvement that lightens the dish considerably. If you'd like a slightly spicy version, add a teaspoon or two of Asian chili sauce along with the other liquid ingredients toward the end of cooking. Use a metal serving spoon, or a knife if necessary, to cut through the crisply browned noodle pancake before serving it with the stir-fried mixture.

¾ pound fresh or ½ pound dried thin Asian egg or wheat noodles

1½ cups peanut or corn oil

¾ pound medium-sized fresh shrimp, peeled and deveined

1 medium-sized garlic clove, chopped fine

1 tablespoon finely grated fresh gingerroot

1 medium-sized green bell pepper, halved, stemmed, seeded, and cut into ½-inch squares

1 medium-sized onion, quartered and cut into ½-inch slices

1 medium-sized carrot, halved lengthwise, then cut diagonally crosswise into ¼-inch-thick slices

1 medium-sized firm, ripe tomato, cored and cut into thin wedges

½ cup coarsely chopped fresh or drained canned pineapple

½ cup chicken broth

¼ cup sugar

¼ cup rice vinegar

2 tablespoons light soy sauce

1 tablespoon cornstarch

1 tablespoon coarsely chopped fresh cilantro or thinly sliced scallion

Bring a large pan of water to a boil, add the noodles, and cook until tender. Drain, rinse under cold running water, and drain well again.

In a heavy medium-sized skillet, heat 1¼ cups of the oil over moderate heat. Add the drained noodles, using a wooden spatula or spoon to spread them evenly and press them gently, forming an even, loose cake. Fry until their underside is golden brown, 5 to 7 minutes, checking frequently to avoid burning. Then carefully turn the cake over to cook the other side.

A minute or two before turning the noodles, heat half of the remaining oil in a large wok or skillet over high heat. Add the shrimp and stir-fry just until they turn pink, 1 to 2 minutes; remove from the wok and set aside.

Add the remaining oil to the wok along with the garlic and ginger; as soon as they sizzle, add the bell pepper, onion, and carrot, stir-frying about 2 minutes. Add the tomato and pineapple and stir-fry 1 minute more. Add the broth, sugar, and vinegar and stir until the sugar dissolves, stirring and scraping to deglaze. Stir together the soy sauce and cornstarch and add to the wok with the reserved shrimp. Simmer until the liquid thickens to coating consistency, 2 to 3 minutes.

While the liquid simmers, remove the browned noodles from the skillet and drain on paper towels. Transfer to a heated platter and mound the sweet-and-sour mixture on top of the noodles. Garnish with cilantro or scallion.

MAKES 4 SERVINGS

Curried Shrimp Lo Mein

CHINA

A touch of curry powder makes this noodle dish a little bit out of the ordinary. Try it with chicken, too.

1 pound fresh or ¾ pound dried thin to medium-thin Asian wheat or egg noodles

¼ cup peanut or vegetable oil

1 medium-sized garlic clove, chopped fine

1 tablespoon grated fresh gingerroot

¾ pound fresh small to medium-sized shrimp, shelled and deveined

2 teaspoons mild curry powder

4 medium-sized leaves bok choy or Nappa cabbage, cut crosswise into ½-inch-wide pieces

¼ cup chicken broth

1 tablespoon light soy sauce

1 tablespoon dry sherry

½ teaspoon sugar

¼ cup finely chopped fresh cilantro

Bring a large pan of water to a boil, add the noodles, and cook until tender. Drain well, transfer to a bowl, and toss with half of the oil until well coated. Set aside.

In a large wok or skillet, heat 1 tablespoon more of the oil over moderately high heat. Add the garlic and ginger; as soon as they sizzle, add the shrimp and stir-fry just until they begin to turn pink, about 1 minute. Sprinkle with the curry powder, add the bok choy or cabbage, and stir-fry 1 minute more. Remove from the wok and set aside.

Heat the remaining oil in the wok. Add the reserved noodles and let them sit until slightly browned, about 1 minute. Then return the reserved shrimp mixture to the wok, add the broth, soy sauce, sherry, and sugar and continue stir-frying until the liquid has been almost completely absorbed or evaporated, 5 to 7 minutes. Garnish with cilantro.

MAKES 4 SERVINGS

Noodles with Spicy Minced Chicken, Mushrooms, and Black-Bean Sauce

❧

This noodle dish is a lunchtime favorite in Chinese noodle shops, its simple topping of ground chicken enriched with meaty *shiitake* mushrooms and dark Asian sesame oil pressed from toasted seeds. Try substituting ground pork or even ground lamb for the chicken.

1 pound fresh or ¾ pound dried chow mein *or other thin Asian egg or wheat noodles*
¼ cup peanut oil
4 medium-sized garlic cloves, chopped fine
2 tablespoons grated fresh gingerroot
1¼ pounds ground chicken
12 dried shiitake *mushrooms, soaked in warm water until soft, rinsed well, stems trimmed off and discarded, caps coarsely chopped*

⅓ cup sesame seeds
1 cup bottled Chinese black-bean sauce
3 tablespoons hot chili oil
3 tablespoons rice vinegar
2 tablespoons light soy sauce
Salt and white pepper
1 tablespoon Asian sesame oil
½ cup thinly sliced fresh scallions

Bring a large pan of water to a boil and cook the noodles until tender.

Meanwhile, in a wok or skillet, heat the peanut oil over moderately high heat. Add the garlic and ginger and stir-fry for 1 minute. Add the chicken, mushrooms, and sesame seeds and stir-fry, breaking up the chicken, until it just begins to brown, 5 to 7 minutes.

Add the black-bean sauce, chili oil, rice vinegar, and soy sauce. Simmer, stirring, until the mixture is thick and uniformly heated, 2 to 3 minutes. Season to taste with salt and white pepper.

Drain the noodles, toss them briefly with the sesame oil, and arrange on a serving platter or four individual plates, mounding the noodles slightly. Spoon the sauce on top of the noodles and garnish with scallions.

MAKES 4 SERVINGS

Pan-Fried Noodles with Stir-Fried Ginger Chicken and Broccoli

CHINA

This is a classic topping combination for pan-fried noodles. Use a metal serving spoon, or a knife if necessary, to cut through the crisply browned noodle pancake before serving it with the stir-fried mixture.

> ¾ pound fresh or ½ pound dried thin
>   Asian egg or wheat noodles
> 1½ cups peanut or corn oil
> 1 medium-sized garlic clove, chopped fine
> 1 tablespoon grated fresh gingerroot
> 1½ cups small broccoli florets
> ¾ pound boneless skinless chicken breasts,
>   cut crosswise into ¼-inch-thick slices
> 1¼ cups chicken broth
> ¼ cup light soy sauce
> 1½ tablespoons cornstarch
> 1 teaspoon sugar
> 2 medium-sized scallions, sliced thin

Bring a large pan of water to a boil, add the noodles, and cook until tender. Drain, rinse under cold running water, and drain well again.

In a heavy medium-sized skillet, heat 1¼ cups of the oil over moderate heat. Add the drained noodles, using a wooden spatula or spoon to spread them evenly and press them gently, forming an even, loose cake. Fry until their underside is golden brown, 5 to 7 minutes, checking frequently to avoid burning. Then carefully turn the cake over to cook the other side.

A minute or two before turning the noodles, heat the remaining oil in a large wok or skillet over high heat. Add the garlic and ginger; as soon as they sizzle, add the broccoli and stir-fry until it turns bright green, 1 to 2 minutes. Remove it from the wok and add the chicken, stir-frying until it turns golden, about 5 minutes. Return the broccoli to the wok and add the broth, stirring and scraping to deglaze. Stir together the soy sauce, cornstarch, and sugar and, as soon as the liquid in the wok simmers, stir in the mixture. Continue simmering until the liquid thickens to coat the chicken and broccoli, 2 to 3 minutes.

While the liquid simmers, remove the browned noodles from the skillet and drain on paper towels. Transfer to a heated platter and mound the chicken-and-broccoli mixture on top of the noodles. Garnish with scallions.

MAKES 4 SERVINGS

Pan-Fried Noodles with Stir-Fried Chicken and Leeks

CHINA

The mild, sweet, yet distinctively oniony flavor of the leeks and their almost melting texture when stir-fried nicely complement the chicken. Use a metal serving spoon, or a knife if necessary, to cut through the crisply browned noodle pancake before serving it with the stir-fried mixture.

*¾ pound fresh or ½ pound dried thin
    Asian egg or wheat noodles*
1½ cups peanut or corn oil
*2 medium-sized leeks, root ends and dark
    green tips trimmed off, leeks halved
    lengthwise, thoroughly washed, and cut
    crosswise into ¼-inch-thick slices*
*¾ pound boneless skinless chicken breasts,
    cut crosswise into ¼-inch-thick slices*
1¼ cups chicken broth
¼ cup light soy sauce
2 tablespoons rice vinegar
1½ tablespoons cornstarch
*1 tablespoon coarsely chopped fresh
    cilantro*

Bring a large pan of water to a boil, add the noodles, and cook until tender. Drain, rinse under cold running water, and drain well again.

In a heavy medium-sized skillet, heat 1¼ cups of the oil over moderate heat. Add the drained noodles, using a wooden spatula or spoon to spread them evenly and press them gently, forming an even, loose cake. Fry until their underside is golden brown, 5 to 7 minutes, checking frequently to avoid burning. Then carefully turn the cake over to cook the other side.

A minute or two before turning the noodles, heat the remaining oil in a large wok or skillet over high heat. Add the leeks and stir-fry about 1 minute. Add the chicken, stir-frying until it turns golden, about 5 minutes. Add the broth, stirring and scraping to deglaze. Stir together the soy sauce, rice vinegar, and cornstarch; as soon as the liquid in the wok simmers, stir in the mixture. Continue simmering until the liquid thickens to coat the chicken and leeks, 2 to 3 minutes.

While the liquid simmers, remove the browned noodles from the skillet and drain on paper towels. Transfer to a heated platter and mound the chicken-and-leek mixture on top of the noodles. Garnish with cilantro.

MAKES 4 SERVINGS

Szechuan Chicken Lo Mein with Cilantro Sauce

CHINA

A pesto-like mixture of fresh cilantro, chicken broth, soy sauce, and chili oil coats the chicken and noodles in this somewhat out-of-the-ordinary version of *lo mein*.

1 pound fresh or ¾ pound dried thin to medium-thin Asian wheat or egg noodles
¼ cup peanut or vegetable oil
⅓ cup packed fresh cilantro leaves
¼ cup chicken broth
2 tablespoons light soy sauce
1 tablespoon hot chili oil

1 tablespoon dry sherry
½ teaspoon sugar
2 medium-sized garlic cloves, chopped fine
1 tablespoon grated fresh gingerroot
¾ pound boneless skinless chicken breasts, cut crosswise into ¼-inch-thick slices

Bring a large pan of water to a boil, add the noodles, and cook until tender. Drain well, transfer to a bowl, and toss with half of the peanut or vegetable oil until well coated. Set aside.

Put the cilantro, broth, soy sauce, chili oil, sherry, and sugar in a food processor with the metal blade. Pulse the machine several times, then process until the cilantro is finely chopped and the mixture smoothly blended.

In a large wok or skillet, heat 1 tablespoon more of the oil over moderately high heat. Add the garlic and ginger; as soon as they sizzle, add the chicken and stir-fry until it just begins to brown, 3 to 5 minutes. Remove from the wok and set aside.

Heat the remaining oil in the wok. Add the reserved noodles and let them sit until slightly browned, about 1 minute. Then return the reserved chicken to the wok, add the cilantro mixture, and continue stir-frying until the liquid has been almost completely absorbed or evaporated, 5 to 7 minutes.

MAKES 4 SERVINGS

Barbecued Pork Lo Mein

CHINA

This is a classic version of Chinese stir-fried noodles. If you can't find Chinese barbecued pork, known as *char sui*—the kind sold in Asian markets and Chinese takeouts—substitute a good-quality, fairly sweet smoked ham for a similarly rich flavor.

1 pound fresh or ¾ pound dried thin to
   medium-thin Asian wheat or egg noodles
¼ cup peanut or vegetable oil
1 medium-sized garlic clove, chopped fine
1½ tablespoons grated fresh gingerroot
¾ pound Chinese barbecued pork, cut
   into ¼- by 1-inch pieces
2 medium-sized scallions, cut into 1-inch shreds
1 medium-sized carrot, cut into ⅛-inch
   by 1- to 2-inch matchsticks
¼ cup chicken broth
2 tablespoons light soy sauce
1 tablespoon dry sherry
½ teaspoon sugar

Bring a large pan of water to a boil, add the noodles, and cook until tender. Drain well, transfer to a bowl, and toss with half of the oil until well coated. Set aside.

In a large wok or skillet, heat 1 tablespoon more of the oil over moderately high heat. Add the garlic and ginger; as soon as they sizzle, add the pork, scallions, and carrot and stir-fry about 1 minute. Remove from the wok and set aside.

Heat the remaining oil in the wok. Add the reserved noodles and let them sit until slightly browned, about 1 minute. Then return the reserved pork mixture to the wok, add the broth, soy sauce, sherry, and sugar and continue stir-frying until the liquid has been almost completely absorbed or evaporated, 5 to 7 minutes.

MAKES 4 SERVINGS

Pan-Fried Noodles with Stir-Fried Beef and Tomatoes

CHINA

Although native to the Americas, tomatoes have long since found their way into the Chinese kitchen—most notably in slightly sweet-sour stir-fries such as this classic. Use a metal serving spoon, or a knife if necessary, to cut through the crisply browned noodle pancake before serving it with the stir-fried mixture.

¾ pound fresh or ½ pound dried thin
Asian egg or wheat noodles
1½ cups peanut or corn oil
2 medium-sized garlic cloves, chopped
fine
1 tablespoon finely grated fresh
gingerroot
¾ pound lean beef steak, well trimmed
and cut crosswise into ¼-inch-thick
slices
3 medium-sized firm, ripe tomatoes,
cored and cut into thin wedges
1 cup beef or chicken broth
¼ cup light soy sauce
1½ tablespoons cornstarch
1 tablespoon rice vinegar
1 tablespoon Worcestershire sauce
1 tablespoon sugar
1 tablespoon coarsely chopped fresh
cilantro

Bring a large pan of water to a boil, add the noodles, and cook until tender. Drain, rinse under cold running water, and drain well again.

In a heavy medium-sized skillet, heat 1¼ cups of the oil over moderate heat. Add the drained noodles, using a wooden spatula or spoon to spread them evenly and press them gently, forming an even, loose cake. Fry until their underside is golden brown, 5 to 7 minutes, checking frequently to avoid burning. Then carefully turn the cake over to cook the other side.

A minute or two before turning the noodles, heat the remaining oil in a large wok or skillet over high heat. Add the garlic and ginger; as soon as they sizzle, add the beef, stir-frying until it loses its pink color and the edges begin to brown, about 5 minutes. Add the tomatoes and stir-fry 1 minute more. Add the broth, stirring and scraping to deglaze. Stir together the soy sauce, cornstarch, rice vinegar, Worcestershire sauce, and sugar; as soon as the liquid in the wok simmers, stir in the mixture. Continue simmering until the liquid thickens to coat the beef and tomatoes, 2 to 3 minutes.

While the liquid simmers, remove the browned noodles from the skillet and drain on paper towels. Transfer to a heated platter and mound the beef-and-tomato mixture on top of the noodles. Garnish with cilantro.

MAKES 4 SERVINGS

Beef Lo Mein with Mixed Vegetables

CHINA

Feel free to elaborate this dish with your favorite vegetable or to substitute another kind of inexpensive steak.

1 pound fresh or ¾ pound dried thin to
  medium-thin Asian wheat or egg
  noodles
⅓ cup peanut or vegetable oil
2 medium-sized garlic cloves, chopped
  fine
2 medium-sized scallions, sliced thin
1 tablespoon grated fresh gingerroot
2 medium-sized carrots, cut diagonally
  into ¼-inch-thick slices
1 medium-sized onion, halved and sliced
  thin
¼ pound small snow peas, trimmed
¼ pound mushrooms, cut into quarters or
  halves depending on size
¾ pound beef flank steak, cut crosswise
  into ¼-inch-thick slices
¼ cup chicken broth
2 tablespoons light soy sauce
1 tablespoon dry sherry
½ teaspoon salt

Bring a large pan of water to a boil, add the noodles, and cook until tender. Drain well, transfer to a bowl, and toss with 2 tablespoons of the oil until well coated. Set aside.

In a large wok or skillet, heat 1 tablespoon more of the oil over moderately high heat. Add the garlic, scallions, and ginger; as soon as they sizzle, add the carrots and onion and stir-fry about 1 minute; add the snow peas and mushrooms and sauté 1 to 2 minutes more, until the vegetables are tender-crisp. Remove from the wok and set aside.

Heat 2 tablespoons more of the oil in the wok. Add the beef and stir-fry until it begins to brown, 3 to 5 minutes. Remove from the wok and set aside.

Heat the remaining oil in the wok. Add the reserved noodles and let them sit until slightly browned, about 1 minute. Then return the reserved vegetables and the reserved beef to the wok. Add the broth, soy sauce, sherry, and salt and continue stir-frying until the liquid has been almost completely absorbed or evaporated, 5 to 7 minutes.

MAKES 4 SERVINGS

2
${\mathcal E}$UROPEAN AND AMERICAN EGG NOODLES

Though Italy's dried and fresh pastas are perhaps best known throughout Europe and North America, other European-based cuisines have their own indigenous noodles and noodle dishes. For the most part, these are based on egg-enriched wheat doughs, usually rolled out and cut to form ribbons ranging from thin strands resembling Italian angel-hair pasta to broad noodles as wide as lasagna.

Virtually all European cuisines have their own traditional, sometimes painstaking methods for preparing fresh egg noodles, as well as thicker egg-and-flour mixtures that yield boiled or steamed dumplings. But, as the recipes in this chapter show, a vast range of recipes rely on the widely available dried egg noodles found in supermarkets, food stores, and delicatessens everywhere. Feel free, if you like, to substitute fresh egg noodles found in the refrigerated case of many markets, using in any given recipe about 30 percent more fresh noodles by weight than the measurement called for of dried noodles.

All ready-made noodles are exceedingly easy to cook, requiring relatively brief boiling (the actual time depends on their size and is indicated on the manufacturer's packaging) in a large quantity of usually salted boiling water. Take some care, however, in the timing of your recipe when using dried or fresh egg noodles. Once cooked, they tend to stick together and should be mixed with sauce or other ingredients as soon as possible after cooking.

Chicken Soup with Lockshen

❧

Thin egg noodles—known by the Yiddish word *lockshen*—are one of the most satisfying embellishments to a bowl of chicken broth. Unless you feel inclined to make your own broth from scratch, use the best-quality canned or frozen broth you can find. This recipe adds more flavor to it through a brief simmering with aromatic vegetables.

> 2 quarts chicken broth
> 2 medium-sized carrots, cut into ½-inch-
> thick slices
> 2 medium-sized celery stalks, cut into
> ½-inch-thick slices
> 2 small onions, quartered
> 1 medium-sized leek, trimmed, split in
> half lengthwise, thoroughly washed,
> and cut into ½-inch-thick slices
> 1 bay leaf
> ½ pound thin dried egg noodles
> Salt
> 1 tablespoon finely chopped fresh parsley

—42—

Put the broth in a saucepan with the carrots, celery, onions, leek, and bay leaf. Bring to a boil over moderate heat; reduce the heat to low and simmer gently, partially covered, for about 30 minutes.

Meanwhile, bring a medium-sized saucepan of water to a boil. Add the noodles and a sprinkling of salt and boil until the noodles are al dente. Drain well.

Pour the broth through a cheesecloth-lined strainer to remove the vegetables and any impurities from the broth. Return it to the pan and gently rewarm. Distribute the noodles among four individual bowls, adding a few carrot and celery slices if you like. Ladle the hot broth over the noodles and garnish with parsley.

MAKES 4 SERVINGS

Egg Noodles with Browned Breadcrumbs and Almonds

❧

If you like, add Parmesan cheese to taste to this side dish to transform it into a simple main course.

> ¾ pound medium dried egg noodles
> Salt
> 1¼ cups unsalted butter, cut into pieces
> ½ cup slivered almonds
> 1 cup fine dry breadcrumbs
> Black pepper
> 2 tablespoons finely chopped fresh
>   parsley

—43—

Bring a medium-sized saucepan of water to a boil. Add the noodles and a sprinkling of salt and boil until the noodles are al dente, following package instructions.

Meanwhile, melt the butter in a large skillet over moderate heat. As soon as the butter begins to foam, add the almonds. Sauté until they just begin to turn golden, about 1 minute. Add the breadcrumbs and sauté until golden brown, about 2 minutes more.

Drain the noodles well and add them to the skillet. Toss well to coat them, seasoning to taste with black pepper. Transfer to a serving dish and garnish with parsley.

MAKES 4 SERVINGS

Pan-Browned Noodles with Caramelized Onions

FRANCE

Onions, slowly cooked until their natural sugars caramelize, develop a rich, mellow sweetness that is perfectly complemented by boiled egg noodles. Serve this alongside roast or grilled meats or poultry.

½ cup unsalted butter
4 medium-sized onions, sliced thin
Salt
½ pound medium to wide dried egg
    noodles
Black pepper
1 tablespoon finely chopped fresh parsley
1 tablespoon finely chopped fresh chives

In a large saucepan, melt 6 tablespoons of the butter over low heat. Add the onions, sprinkle to taste with salt, and stir well. Cover and cook, stirring occasionally, until the onions are very tender, about 20 minutes.

Remove the cover, raise the heat slightly, and sauté the onions, stirring frequently to avoid scorching, until they turn a deep caramel brown, about 45 minutes.

Meanwhile, bring a medium-sized saucepan of water to a boil. Add the noodles and a sprinkling of salt and boil until the noodles are al dente, following package instructions. Drain well.

As soon as the onions are caramelized, add the drained noodles and remaining butter to the pan and stir gently to combine the noodles and onions. Season to taste with salt and pepper. Transfer to a serving dish and garnish with parsley and chives.

MAKES 4 SERVINGS

Kasha Varnishkes

RUSSIA

Whenever I order this in a deli, I'm always surprised by how something so basic and simple—a combination of steamed buckwheat groats and egg noodles—can taste so good and be so satisfying. If you want a particularly attractive version, try it with bow-tie-shaped noodles.

1 cup buckwheat groats
3 cups chicken broth
½ pound medium dried egg noodles
Salt
2 tablespoons unsalted butter
2 tablespoons vegetable oil
1 medium-sized onion, chopped coarse
1 medium-sized scallion, sliced thin

Put the buckwheat groats in a nonstick saucepan over moderate heat. Stirring frequently, cook the groats until they are lightly browned and give off a toasty, slightly sour aroma, 7 to 10 minutes.

Add the broth, bring to a boil, reduce the heat to very low, cover, and simmer gently until the buckwheat has absorbed all the liquid and is tender, 20 to 30 minutes. If the buckwheat seems dry before it is fully cooked, add a little boiling water to the pan.

Meanwhile, bring a medium-sized saucepan of water to a boil. Add the noodles and a sprinkling of salt and boil until the noodles are al dente, following package instructions.

While the noodles and buckwheat are cooking, heat the butter and oil in a large skillet over moderate heat. Add the onion and sauté until evenly browned, 5 to 7 minutes. Drain the noodles well and add them to the skillet with the kasha. Stir well to mix. Transfer to a serving bowl and garnish with scallion.

MAKES 4 SERVINGS

Egg Ribbons with Four Cheeses

The crossroads of Europe draws on its own and neighboring cheeses for this richly flavored noodle dish.

> ½ pound medium to wide dried egg
>   noodles
> Salt
> 2½ cups heavy cream
> ¼ pound Gruyère cheese, shredded
> ¼ pound Gorgonzola cheese, crumbled
> ¼ pound ripe Camembert or Brie cheese,
>   white rinds trimmed and discarded
> ½ cup grated Parmesan cheese

Bring a medium-sized saucepan of water to a boil. Add the noodles and a sprinkling of salt and boil until the noodles are al dente, following package instructions.

Meanwhile, put the cream in another medium-sized saucepan over moderate heat. As soon as it is hot but not yet boiling, 3 to 4 minutes, stir in the Gruyère and Gorgonzola. Then add the Camembert or Brie, pinching off and dropping in small clumps with your fingers. Finally, sprinkle and stir in the Parmesan.

Raise the heat slightly and bring the sauce to a boil, stirring constantly. Reduce the heat and simmer gently until the sauce is thick and creamy, about 5 minutes.

Drain the noodles and put them in a serving bowl. Pour the sauce on top and toss well before serving.

MAKES 4 SERVINGS

Spinach Noodles with Cheese and Herbs

FRANCE

Egg noodles flavored and colored with spinach taste and look particularly striking when partnered with a simple sauce made from one of the garlic-and-herb-flavored French triple-cream cheeses, such as the widely known Boursin brand. Of course, you also can make this recipe with regular egg noodles.

> ½ pound medium to wide spinach egg
>   noodles
> Salt
> ½ cup heavy cream
> 3 (5-ounce) packages triple-cream cheese
>   with garlic and fines herbes, at room
>   temperature
> ¼ cup finely chopped fresh chives
> ¼ cup finely chopped fresh parsley
> Black pepper

Bring a medium-sized saucepan of water to a boil. Add the noodles and a sprinkling of salt and boil until the noodles are al dente, following package instructions.

Meanwhile, put the cream in another medium-sized saucepan over moderate heat. As soon as it is hot but not yet boiling, 3 to 4 minutes, add the cheese, breaking it up into small clumps with your fingers as you put it in the pan. Stir just until the cheese melts.

Drain the noodles well and add them and the chives and parsley to the sauce in the pan. Toss well and season to taste with pepper. Serve immediately.

MAKES 4 SERVINGS

Noodles Romanoff au Gratin

The glory days of Imperial Russia give us this luxurious baked noodle side dish, ideal with meat or poultry main courses.

½ pound medium to wide dried egg
 noodles
Salt
½ cup unsalted butter, at room
 temperature
⅔ cup fine fresh white breadcrumbs
2 cups sour cream
2 cups freshly grated Parmesan cheese
White pepper

Preheat the oven to 350°F.

Bring a medium-sized saucepan of water to a boil. Add the noodles and a sprinkling of salt and boil until the noodles are al dente, following package instructions.

Meanwhile, melt half of the butter in a medium-sized skillet over moderate heat. Add the breadcrumbs and sauté until lightly browned, 2 to 3 minutes. Set aside.

In a mixing bowl, stir together the sour cream, Parmesan cheese, and salt and white pepper to taste. Drain the noodles well and add them to the bowl, stirring to mix well.

Grease a baking dish with the remaining butter and add the noodles. Spread the reserved breadcrumbs evenly on top. Bake until hot and bubbly, 10 to 15 minutes.

MAKES 4 SERVINGS

Noodles with Stilton and Port Cream and Toasted Walnuts

Great British flavors join together to make this a most luxurious noodle preparation. Substitute another creamy blue-veined cheese for the Stilton, if necessary. Try toasted hazelnuts instead of the walnuts.

3 cups heavy cream
½ cup port wine
1½ pounds Stilton cheese, crumbled
¾ pound wide dried egg noodles
Salt
¼ cup unsalted butter
1½ cups shelled walnut pieces, toasted
  (see Index)
2 tablespoons finely chopped fresh chives

—49—

In a large saucepan, bring the cream to a boil over high heat. Add the port, reduce the heat slightly, and boil gently until reduced by about ½ cup, 7 to 10 minutes. Crumble in the Stilton cheese and continue simmering until it has melted and the sauce is thickened, about 5 minutes more.

Meanwhile, bring a medium-sized saucepan of water to a boil. Add the noodles and a sprinkling of salt and boil until the noodles are al dente, following package instructions. Drain well.

In the saucepan you used for the noodles, melt the butter over moderate heat. Add the walnuts and noodles and toss well.

Transfer the noodles to a serving bowl or four individual plates and ladle the sauce on top. Garnish with chives.

MAKES 4 SERVINGS

Old-Fashioned Macaroni and Cheese

UNITED STATES

❧

Where would the average American dinner table be without it? This version is at once both simplified and enriched by replacing the usual flour-thickened sauce with a reduction of heavy cream. A combination of mild cheddar and Parmesan cheeses adds extra flavor. You can use either elbow macaroni or ribbon-shaped egg noodles. If you want to make it more interesting, add some slivers of ham or ribbons of fresh spinach leaves to the sauce just before adding the noodles.

4 cups heavy cream
¾ pound elbow macaroni or wide dried
  egg noodles
Salt
1½ pounds mild cheddar cheese, shredded
¾ cup grated Parmesan cheese
White pepper

In a medium-sized saucepan, bring the cream to a boil over high heat. Reduce the heat slightly and gently boil, stirring occasionally, until reduced by about one-third, 10 to 15 minutes.

Meanwhile, bring a medium-sized saucepan of water to a boil. Add the noodles and a sprinkling of salt and boil until the noodles are al dente, following package instructions. Drain well.

Stirring continuously, sprinkle the cheddar and Parmesan cheeses into the reduced cream until they melt. Season to taste with salt and white pepper, add the drained noodles, and transfer to a serving bowl or four individual plates.

MAKES 4 SERVINGS

Farmer's Noodles

I like to think of this recipe, served at room temperature, as an Eastern European ancestor of today's popular pasta salads. My grandmother, who was born in Belorussia, used to make a version of it for lunch. Add or substitute whatever fresh vegetables you like.

¾ pound medium dried egg noodles
Salt
14 ounces hoop cheese or farmer cheese,
    at room temperature
½ cup plain low-fat yogurt
⅓ cup grated Parmesan cheese
8 medium-sized radishes, grated coarse
1 medium-sized carrot, shredded coarse
1 large pickling cucumber, shredded
    coarse
1 medium-sized red or green bell pepper,
    stemmed, seeded, grated coarse
1 small red onion, chopped fine
2 tablespoons coarsely chopped fresh
    parsley
2 tablespoons coarsely chopped fresh
    chives
Salt and black pepper

—51—

Bring a medium-sized saucepan of water to a boil. Add the noodles and a sprinkling of salt and boil until the noodles are al dente. Drain well.

In a mixing bowl, mash together the hoop or farmer cheese, yogurt, and Parmesan cheese. Stir in the radishes, carrot, cucumber, bell pepper, onion, parsley, and chives. Add the noodles, toss well, and season to taste with salt and pepper.

MAKES 4 SERVINGS

Egg Noodles with Wild Mushroom Cream

FRANCE

The wild mushrooms known as *cepes* in France and *porcini* in Italy—and worldwide by the scientific name *boletus edulus*—have one of the richest, sweetest, earthiest flavors in the mushroom kingdom. Available year-round in their dried form, they are costly indeed; but a little goes a long way, as this French-style noodle-dish demonstrates. Serve it as an appetizer or a luxurious main course.

1½ ounces dried cepes or porcini
1 cup dry white wine
¼ cup unsalted butter
4 large shallots, chopped fine
3 cups heavy cream
¾ pound medium dried egg noodles
Salt and white pepper
2 tablespoons finely chopped fresh parsley

Put the mushrooms in a bowl and cover with the wine. Leave them to soak until soft, 10 to 15 minutes. Remove the mushrooms from the bowl, chop them coarsely, and set aside. Line a small sieve with cheesecloth and pour the wine through to strain out any grit or other impurities; set the wine aside.

In a medium-sized skillet melt the butter over moderate heat. Add the shallots and sauté until tender, 2 to 3 minutes. Add the reserved mushrooms and sauté 1 minute more.

Add the reserved wine, raise the heat slightly, and simmer for 1 minute. Add the cream and gently boil until the sauce is thick and reduced by half, about 20 minutes.

Meanwhile, bring a medium-sized saucepan of water to a boil. Add the noodles and a sprinkling of salt and boil until the noodles are al dente, following package instructions. Drain well.

When the sauce is done, taste and adjust the seasonings with salt and white pepper. Add the noodles, toss well, and transfer to a serving bowl. Garnish with parsley.

MAKES 4 SERVINGS

Egg Noodles with Spiced Cottage Cheese and Sour Cream

HUNGARY

Rich and flavorful, this peasant-style dish is quickly assembled and intensely satisfying.

1 pound wide dried egg noodles
Salt
4 tablespoons unsalted butter
1 small onion, chopped fine
1 small garlic clove, chopped fine
½ cup poppy seeds
¼ cup caraway seeds
2 cups large-curd cottage cheese, at room
   temperature
1 cup sour cream
Paprika
2 tablespoons finely chopped fresh chives

—53—

Bring a large saucepan of water to a boil. Add the noodles and a sprinkling of salt and boil until tender, following package instructions.

A few minutes before the noodles are done, melt the butter in another large saucepan over moderate heat. Add the onion and garlic and sauté until translucent, 2 to 3 minutes. Add the poppy and caraway seeds and sauté 1 minute more.

As soon as the noodles are done, drain them well.

Add the cottage cheese and sour cream to the poppy-and-caraway-seed mixture and stir to blend. Then add the drained noodles and toss gently just until well mixed, generously seasoning to taste with salt. Transfer to a heated serving bowl; dust generously with paprika and garnish with chives.

MAKES 4 SERVINGS

Tuna and Noodle Casserole with Mushrooms

UNITED STATES

If you really must, you could take the well-known shortcut of using canned soup. But you'll miss out on the unmistakably rich, earthy flavor of fresh mushrooms that suffuses this classic noodle casserole. Substitute leftover chicken or turkey for the tuna, if you wish.

2 tablespoons vegetable oil
¼ cup unsalted butter, at room
   temperature
1 medium-sized onion, sliced thin
1 medium-sized garlic clove, chopped fine
1 pound fresh mushrooms, chopped fine
2 tablespoons all-purpose flour
2½ cups half-and-half
¾ pound wide dried egg noodles
Salt
¼ teaspoon sweet paprika
White pepper
2 (6½-ounce) cans tuna, drained and
   flaked coarse
¾ cup grated Parmesan cheese
2 tablespoons finely chopped fresh
   parsley
2 tablespoons finely chopped fresh chives
¾ cup slivered almonds

In a medium-sized saucepan, heat the oil and half of the butter over moderate heat. Add the onion and garlic and sauté until they just begin to brown, about 5 minutes. Add the mushrooms, raise the heat, and sauté, stirring frequently, until they cook down to a thick, dark-brown paste, 15 to 20 minutes. About halfway through the cooking time, sprinkle in the flour and stir well.

Add the half-and-half and stir to dissolve the pan deposits. Simmer, stirring occasionally, until thick, about 15 minutes more.

Preheat the oven to 350°F.

Meanwhile, bring a medium-sized saucepan of water to a boil. Add the noodles and a sprinkling of salt and boil until the noodles are al dente, following package instructions. Drain well.

Stir the paprika into the sauce, taste, and adjust the seasonings with salt and white pepper. Stir in the tuna, Parmesan cheese, noodles, parsley, and chives.

Grease a baking dish with the remaining butter and fill it with the noodle mixture. Top with almonds. Bake until the mixture is hot and bubbly and the almonds are golden, 15 to 20 minutes.

MAKES 4 SERVINGS

Chicken a la King with Noodles

UNITED STATES

A classic old-fashioned family supper utilizing leftover chicken, this recipe also can be made with turkey or tuna.

¼ cup unsalted butter
1 medium-sized onion, chopped fine
1 medium-sized garlic clove, chopped fine
1 medium-sized celery stalk, sliced thin
¼ cup all-purpose flour
1 cup chicken broth
1 cup half-and-half
¾ pound medium to wide dried egg
    noodles
Salt
1 egg yolk, beaten
3 cups cooked chicken, cut into ½-inch
    chunks
1 medium-sized red bell pepper, halved,
    stemmed, seeded, and cut into ¼-inch
    squares
1 medium-sized green bell pepper,
    halved, stemmed, seeded (see Index),
    and cut into ¼-inch squares
¾ cup cooked fresh or frozen peas
⅛ teaspoon grated nutmeg
White pepper
2 tablespoons finely chopped fresh
    parsley
2 tablespoons finely chopped fresh chives

In a large saucepan, melt the butter over moderately low heat. Add the onion, garlic, and celery and sauté until tender, 2 to 3 minutes. Sprinkle in the flour and sauté, stirring continuously, about 1 minute more.

Stirring briskly with a wire whisk, gradually pour in the broth and half-and-half. Raise the heat slightly and, stirring occasionally, bring the liquid to a boil. Reduce the heat and simmer gently for about 10 minutes, stirring occasionally.

Meanwhile, bring a medium-sized saucepan of water to a boil. Add the noodles and a sprinkling of salt and boil until the noodles are al dente, following package instructions.

While the noodles are cooking, put the egg yolk in a mixing bowl and, whisking continuously, slowly pour in a ladleful of the hot broth mixture. Stirring the pan of broth continuously, slowly pour in the yolk mixture.

Reduce the heat to low and add the chicken, bell peppers, and peas to the sauce. Simmer about 5 minutes more. Stir in the nutmeg and season to taste with salt and white pepper.

Drain the noodles well, transfer to a serving bowl or four individual plates, and spoon the sauce on top. Garnish with parsley and chives.

MAKES 4 SERVINGS

Baked Egg Noodles with Cheddar and Bacon

ENGLAND

For the fullest flavor, use the best quality aged sharp cheddar cheese you can find.

¼ cup unsalted butter, at room temperature
8 strips smoked bacon, cut crosswise into
   ¼-inch-wide strips
¼ cup flour
½ teaspoon dry mustard powder
1½ cups heavy cream
¾ pound wide dried egg noodles
Salt
1 pound sharp cheddar cheese, shredded coarse
White pepper

Melt half of the butter in a large skillet over moderate heat. Add the bacon and sauté until it is fairly crisp, 4 to 5 minutes; remove with a slotted spoon and drain on paper towels. Sprinkle the flour and the mustard powder evenly over the fat in the skillet and sauté, stirring, 1 minute more. Whisking continuously, stir in the cream. Bring to a boil, reduce the heat and simmer, stirring frequently, until the sauce is thick, about 15 minutes.

Preheat the oven to 350°F.

Meanwhile, bring a medium-sized saucepan of water to a boil. Add the noodles and a sprinkling of salt and boil until the noodles are al dente, following package instructions. Drain well.

When the sauce is ready, stir in the cheese. As soon as it melts, add the noodles and bacon and stir to mix well, seasoning to taste with salt and white pepper. Grease a baking dish with the remaining butter and fill with the noodle mixture. Bake until hot and bubbly, about 15 minutes.

MAKES 4 SERVINGS

Noodle Ribbons with Bacon, Cabbage, and Onion

GERMANY

This peasant-style side dish goes well with roast or braised meats.

½ pound medium to wide dried egg
   noodles
Salt
½ medium-sized head savoy cabbage, cut
   into ¼- to ½-inch shreds
2 tablespoons unsalted butter
6 rashers smoked bacon, cut crosswise
   into ¼- to ½-inch pieces
1 medium-sized onion, chopped fine
1 tablespoon caraway seeds
Black pepper
2 tablespoons finely chopped fresh
   parsley

Bring a medium-sized saucepan of water to a boil. Add the noodles and a sprinkling of salt and boil until the noodles are al dente, following package instructions.

Spread the cabbage evenly in the bottom of a strainer. Drain the noodles in the strainer, pouring the boiling water evenly over the cabbage to wilt it slightly. Set the noodles and cabbage aside.

In a large skillet, melt the butter over moderate heat. Add the bacon and sauté until it begins to brown, 2 to 3 minutes. Add the onion and caraway seeds and sauté about 2 minutes more. Add the reserved noodles and cabbage, season to taste with salt and pepper, and continue sautéing, stirring well, until the mixture is heated through and the noodles just begin to brown, 5 to 7 minutes more. Transfer to a serving dish and garnish with parsley.

MAKES 4 SERVINGS

Slumgullion

Back in the 1960s, the mother of one of my best high-school friends used to mix up a big pot of this intriguingly named mess of noodles, sauce, meat, and cheese for us to eat after we returned from football games. By all means, feel free to double or triple the recipe if you want to feed a crowd.

2 tablespoons olive oil
2 medium-sized garlic cloves, chopped fine
1 large onion, chopped fine
½ pound ground beef
½ pound sweet or spicy fresh Italian sausage, casings split and removed
1 (28-ounce) can whole tomatoes
2 tablespoons tomato paste
1 tablespoon dried oregano

1 tablespoon dried basil
½ tablespoon sugar
¾ pound wide dried egg noodles
Salt
1 cup canned pitted black olives, drained
¾ pound mozzarella cheese, cut into ½-inch cubes
¼ cup finely chopped fresh parsley
Black pepper

In a large skillet or saucepan, heat the oil over moderate heat. Add the garlic and onion; sauté until tender, 2 to 3 minutes.

Add the beef and sausage and raise the heat slightly. Sauté, using a wooden spoon to break up the meat into coarse chunks, until it has lost all its pink color, about 10 minutes.

Add the tomatoes, breaking them up with your hands. Stir and scrape the pan with the spoon to dissolve the pan deposits. Stir in the tomato paste, oregano, basil, and sugar. Simmer until the sauce is fairly thick, 15 to 20 minutes.

While the sauce is simmering, bring a medium-sized saucepan of water to a boil. Add the noodles and a sprinkling of salt and boil until the noodles are al dente, following package instructions. Drain well.

Add the noodles to the pan of sauce, along with the olives, mozzarella cheese, and parsley. Stir well to mix and season to taste with salt and pepper. Serve from the pan.

MAKES 4 SERVINGS

Noodle Sauté with Black Forest Ham and Mustard

Though Black Forest ham contributes the richest flavor to this simple, luxurious noodle dish, feel free to substitute your favorite smoked ham.

¾ pound wide dried egg noodles
Salt
¾ cup unsalted butter
¾ pound thinly sliced Black Forest ham,
   cut into ½-inch-wide strips
½ cup heavy cream
1 teaspoon German-style prepared
   mustard
Salt and black pepper

Bring a medium-sized saucepan of water to a boil. Add the noodles and a sprinkling of salt and boil until the noodles are al dente, following package instructions. Drain well.

In a large skillet, melt the butter over moderate heat. Add the ham and sauté 1 minute. Add the noodles and sauté until they just begin to brown, about 5 minutes more.

In a small bowl or cup, stir together the cream and mustard. Add them to the skillet and toss well to coat the noodles and heat the cream mixture through. Taste and adjust the seasoning with salt and pepper.

MAKES 4 SERVINGS

Traditional Jewish Noodle Kugel

Virtually every Jewish community—indeed, every Jewish family—has its own hallowed recipe for the baked noodle pudding known as kugel. This is one of the most basic.

½ pound wide dried egg noodles
Salt
6 tablespoons unsalted butter
2 eggs, beaten
¼ cup sour cream, drained
¼ cup honey, at room temperature
1 teaspoon ground cinnamon
1 teaspoon grated orange zest
1 teaspoon grated lemon zest
⅛ teaspoon nutmeg
½ cup seedless raisins

Preheat the oven to 350°F.

Bring a medium-sized saucepan of water to a boil. Add the noodles and a sprinkling of salt and boil until al dente, following package instructions. Drain well.

In the same pan, melt 4 tablespoons of the butter. Add the noodles and toss with the butter to coat them evenly.

In a mixing bowl, stir together the eggs, sour cream, honey, cinnamon, orange and lemon zests, and nutmeg. Add the noodles and the raisins and stir well to mix.

With the remaining butter, grease a baking dish and fill with the noodle mixture. Bake until the kugel is set and lightly browned, about 30 minutes. Serve hot, warm, or cold, cut into squares.

MAKES 4 SERVINGS

Pork Paprikash with Noodles

HUNGARY

Use hot or sweet paprika, or a mixture, as your taste dictates. Try this recipe with chicken, turkey, or beef, too.

¼ cup unsalted butter

2 tablespoons vegetable oil

1 pound pork tenderloin, cut into ½-inch
   pieces

1 medium-sized red bell pepper,
   quartered, stemmed, seeded, and cut
   crosswise into ¼-inch-wide strips

1 medium-sized onion, chopped fine

½ pound wide dried egg noodles

Salt

2 tablespoons paprika

2 teaspoons caraway seeds

½ cup medium-dry white wine

2 tablespoons lemon juice

1 cup sour cream

1 tablespoon tomato paste

White pepper

1 tablespoon finely chopped fresh chives

In a large skillet or saucepan, melt the butter and oil over moderately high heat. Add the pork, bell pepper, and onion and sauté until the pork is lightly browned and the vegetables are tender-crisp, about 5 minutes.

At the same time, bring a medium-sized saucepan of water to a boil. Add the noodles and a sprinkling of salt and boil until the noodles are al dente, following package instructions.

Meanwhile, add the paprika and caraway seeds to the pork mixture and sauté 1 minute more. Add the wine and lemon juice and bring to a boil, stirring and scraping to dissolve the pan deposits; reduce the heat slightly and simmer gently for about 5 minutes.

Stir in the sour cream and tomato paste, reduce the heat to low, and simmer 2 to 3 minutes more. Taste and adjust the seasoning with salt and white pepper.

Drain the noodles well and put them in a large serving bowl or on four individual plates. Spoon the pork mixture over the noodles and garnish with chives.

MAKES 4 SERVINGS

Noodle Kugel with Cottage Cheese and Dried Fruit

❧

This version of noodle pudding is richly laden with assorted dried fruits. Feel free to vary the ones you include.

½ pound wide dried egg noodles
Salt
6 tablespoons unsalted butter
3 eggs, beaten
½ cup small-curd cottage cheese, drained
3 tablespoons honey, at room temperature
1 tablespoon lemon juice
2 teaspoons ground cinnamon
⅓ cup dried apricots, chopped coarse
⅓ cup dried pitted prunes, chopped
  coarse
⅓ cup dried pineapple, chopped coarse

Preheat the oven to 350°F.

Bring a medium-sized saucepan of water to a boil. Add the noodles and a sprinkling of salt and boil until al dente, following package instructions. Drain well.

In the same pan, melt 4 tablespoons of the butter. Add the noodles and toss with the butter to coat them evenly.

In a mixing bowl, stir together the eggs, cottage cheese, honey, lemon juice, and cinnamon. Add the noodles, apricots, prunes, and pineapple and stir well to mix.

With the remaining butter, grease a baking dish and fill with the noodle mixture. Bake until the kugel is set and lightly browned, about 30 minutes. Serve hot, warm, or cold, cut into squares.

MAKES 4 SERVINGS

Apple-Cinnamon Noodle Kugel
with Sour Cream

GERMANY

Use the plainest, purest commercial applesauce you can find for this naturally sweet noodle pudding.

¾ cup applesauce
½ pound wide dried egg noodles
Salt
6 tablespoons unsalted butter
3 eggs, beaten
¼ pound cream cheese, softened
¼ cup brown sugar
2 teaspoons ground cinnamon

Line a fine-meshed strainer with cheesecloth and pour in the applesauce, letting the excess liquid drip away. Set the applesauce aside.

Preheat the oven to 350°F.

Bring a medium-sized saucepan of water to a boil. Add the noodles and a sprinkling of salt and boil until al dente, following package instructions. Drain well.

In the same pan, melt 4 tablespoons of the butter. Add the noodles and toss with the butter to coat them evenly.

In a mixing bowl, stir together the reserved applesauce, eggs, cream cheese, brown sugar, and cinnamon. Add the noodles and stir well to mix.

With the remaining butter, grease a baking dish and fill with the noodle mixture. Bake until the kugel is set and lightly browned, about 30 minutes. Serve hot, warm, or cold, cut into squares.

MAKES 4 SERVINGS

Noodle and Plum Jam Pudding

Reminiscent of Hungary's beloved plum dumplings, this kugel is enlivened with the sweet-sour flavor of plum jam. Buy the best quality imported variety of jam you can find, preferably with a chunky consistency.

½ pound wide dried egg noodles
Salt
6 tablespoons unsalted butter
2 eggs, beaten
¼ cup sour cream, drained
¼ cup sugar
1 teaspoon ground cinnamon
1 teaspoon pure vanilla extract
½ cup imported plum jam

Preheat the oven to 350°F.

Bring a medium-sized saucepan of water to a boil. Add the noodles and a sprinkling of salt and boil until al dente, following package instructions. Drain well.

In the same pan, melt 4 tablespoons of the butter. Add the noodles and toss with the butter to coat them evenly.

In a mixing bowl, stir together the eggs, sour cream, sugar, cinnamon, and vanilla. Add the noodles and stir well to mix. Add the plum jam and fold it in briefly, leaving thick swirls of the jam in the noodle mixture.

With the remaining butter, grease a baking dish and fill with the noodle mixture. Bake until the kugel is set and lightly browned, about 30 minutes. Serve hot, warm, or cold, cut into squares.

MAKES 4 SERVINGS

Pan-Fried Noodle Pancakes with Apricot Jam and Sour Cream

AUSTRIA

This old-world preparation makes a satisfying weekend breakfast or brunch dish. Feel free to substitute your own favorite jam or preserves.

> *½ pound thin dried egg noodles*
> *Salt*
> *3 eggs, beaten*
> *2 tablespoons sugar*
> *1 teaspoon ground cinnamon*
> *⅛ teaspoon grated nutmeg*
> *6 tablespoons unsalted butter*
> *1 cup apricot jam*
> *1 cup sour cream*

—67—

Bring a medium-sized saucepan of water to a boil. Add the noodles and a sprinkling of salt and boil until the noodles are al dente, following package instructions. Drain well.

In a mixing bowl, stir together the noodles, eggs, sugar, cinnamon, and nutmeg until well mixed.

In a large skillet, melt 2 tablespoons of the butter over moderate heat. With a spoon, drop the noodle mixture into the skillet to form pancakes about 4 inches across and ½- to ¾-inch thick. Sauté until golden brown, 3 to 4 minutes per side. Transfer to a heated platter and keep warm while frying the remainder, melting more butter as necessary.

Serve the pancakes, passing apricot jam and sour cream for guests to garnish individual servings to taste.

MAKES 4 SERVINGS

3
*B*UCKWHEAT NOODLES

Not really a relative of wheat at all, buckwheat is a plant whose soft seeds yield a dark brown, earthy, slightly sour flour used in some Asian countries to make one of the world's most robust-tasting, satisfying noodles.

Buckwheat noodles reach their pinnacle in Japan, where, known by the name *soba*, the thin strands are appreciated in a range of simple dishes that aim to highlight their unique qualities. Most *soba* are made from a mixture of whole-wheat and buckwheat flours, although some are made from buckwheat alone; extra-special varieties may include green tea, giving them a slight green hue and subtle extra flavor, or pale yellow Japanese mountain yam. You'll also find buckwheat noodles in Korea, although these tend to be made with a product that also includes potato starch and other vegetable starches and may more closely resemble bean threads.

Widely available packaged dry in Japanese markets, buckwheat noodles are easily cooked in boiling water. Take care to follow the manufacturer's package directions and do not overcook the noodles; their flavor and texture is best appreciated when they are done al dente—slightly chewy.

Fox Noodle Soup with Tofu

JAPAN

According to Japanese myth, foxes love the taste and texture of slightly sweetened, deep-fried bean curd—hence the name of this tofu-garnished main-course buckwheat-noodle soup. *Mirin*—syrupy Japanese cooking wine—provides the sweetness; buy it in Asian markets or well-stocked supermarkets.

Vegetable oil for deep-frying
½ pound firm Chinese-style tofu,
   drained well on paper towels and cut
   into ¼-inch-thick slices
2 quarts chicken broth
1 tablespoon grated fresh gingerroot
1 tablespoon sugar

1 tablespoon mirin (Japanese rice wine)
2 tablespoons light soy sauce
1 pound dried soba (Japanese buckwheat
   noodles)
2 scallions, trimmed and cut lengthwise
   into 1-inch-long slivers

In a large, heavy skillet, heat 1 to 2 inches of oil over moderate heat until it registers 350°F on a deep-frying thermometer. Carefully add the tofu slices and fry until golden brown, turning them with a wire skimmer, 1 to 2 minutes. Drain on paper towels.

Fill a mixing bowl with hot tap water. Dip the fried tofu in the water to remove excess oil. Return to fresh paper towels to drain again.

In a medium saucepan over moderate heat, combine ⅔ cup of the broth with the ginger, sugar, and *mirin*. Add the fried tofu and simmer until the liquid is absorbed, 10 to 15 minutes. Set aside.

In a medium saucepan, heat the remaining broth with the soy sauce.

At the same time, fill a large saucepan with water and bring to a boil. Add the *soba* and cook until al dente. Drain well.

Mound the noodles in four individual bowls. Cut the reserved tofu slices into triangles or other decorative shapes and arrange on top of the noodles. Garnish with scallions and ladle the hot broth on top.

MAKES 4 SERVINGS

Soba, Spinach, and Eggs in Broth

Think of this as an Asian variation on the classic Italian soup *stracciatella*. The wisps of egg and ribbons of spinach make a flavorful and colorful complement to the dark-colored buckwheat noodles.

> 1 pound dried soba (Japanese buckwheat
>   noodles)
> 2 quarts chicken broth
> 3 eggs, well beaten
> 1 cup packed thinly shredded fresh
>   spinach leaves
> 2 tablespoons light soy sauce

Fill a large saucepan with water and bring to a boil. Add the *soba* and cook until al dente. Drain well.

Meanwhile, in another large saucepan, bring the broth to a boil. Reduce the heat to a bare simmer and, stirring slowly and continually, add the eggs; continue stirring until it forms thin wisps. Add the spinach and stir briefly, just until it wilts. Stir in the soy sauce.

Mound the noodles in four individual serving bowls. Ladle the broth, egg, and spinach mixture over the noodles.

MAKES 4 SERVINGS

—71—

Warm Soba with Poached Chicken and Egg in Broth

A light but satisfying main-course soup for a chilly day.

> *2 quarts chicken broth*
> *¼ cup light soy sauce*
> *1 pound boneless skinless chicken breasts,*
>   *trimmed*
> *1 pound dried* soba *(Japanese buckwheat*
>   *noodles)*
> *2 hard-boiled eggs, cut into ¼-inch-thick*
>   *slices*
> *2 tablespoons thinly sliced scallions*

Put the broth and soy sauce in a large saucepan and bring to a boil. Reduce the heat to a bare simmer, add the chicken breasts, cover, and cook until they are done, about 10 minutes.

Meanwhile, fill another large saucepan with water and bring to a boil. Add the *soba* and cook until al dente. Drain well.

Remove the chicken breasts and cut them lengthwise into ¼-inch-thick slices. Pour the broth through a strainer lined with cheesecloth; return to the pan and gently rewarm.

Mound the noodles in four individual serving bowls and arrange the chicken breasts and egg slices on top. Ladle the broth into the bowls and garnish with scallions.

MAKES 4 SERVINGS

Warm Soba in Gingered Chicken Broth

JAPAN

Soba noodles make a richly satisfying addition to chicken broth subtly spiced with ginger.

> 2 quarts chicken broth
> 4 (¼-inch-thick) slices fresh gingerroot
> 1 pound dried soba (Japanese buckwheat
>   noodles)
> ¼ cup light soy sauce
> 2 tablespoons thinly sliced scallions

Put the broth and ginger in a large saucepan, bring to a boil, reduce the heat, and simmer gently, uncovered, about 10 minutes.

Meanwhile, fill another large saucepan with water and bring to a boil. Add the *soba* and cook until al dente. Drain well.

Mound the noodles in four individual serving bowls. With a slotted spoon, remove and discard the ginger from the broth; stir in the soy sauce. Ladle the broth over the noodles and garnish with scallions.

MAKES 4 SERVINGS

Cold Soba with Soy and Rice Vinegar Dipping Sauce

JAPAN

This minimalist buckwheat noodle dish, ideal for a light warm-weather lunch, dramatically highlights *soba*'s earthy, slightly sour flavor and chewy texture. Dip small clusters of the noodles into the sauce; or, if you prefer, pour the sauce directly over the noodles.

> 1 pound dried soba (Japanese buckwheat
>   noodles)
> ¾ cup light soy sauce
> ¾ cup rice vinegar
> 3 tablespoons thinly sliced scallions
> 1½ tablespoons grated fresh gingerroot
> 12 ice cubes

Fill a large saucepan with water and bring to a boil. Add the *soba* and cook until al dente. Thoroughly drain, rinsing under cold running water until cool and draining well once again.

In a mixing bowl, stir together the soy sauce, rice vinegar, scallions, and ginger.

Mound the noodles in four individual serving bowls and place 3 ice cubes on top of each mound. Pour the dipping sauce into small bowls or cups to serve alongside each portion of noodles.

MAKES 4 SERVINGS

Cold Soba with Tofu and Seaweed

JAPAN

Three distinctively Japanese ingredients play off each other in this warm-weather light-luncheon main course. Their flavors and textures are harmonized by such distinctive Japanese seasonings as rich and aromatic dried bonito flakes, syrupy-sweet *mirin* cooking wine, and spicy-hot *wasabi* horseradish; along with the noodles, tofu, and sheets of dry *nori* seaweed, these ingredients are available in Japanese markets and large supermarkets.

¾ *cup water*
¼ *cup dried bonito flakes*
½ *cup light soy sauce*
½ *cup* mirin *(Japanese rice wine)*
1 *tablespoon sugar*
1 *pound dried* soba *(Japanese buckwheat noodles)*
½ *pound firm Chinese-style tofu, chilled and cut into* ½*-inch cubes*

2 *sheets* nori *(dried Japanese seaweed), halved, stacked, and cut crosswise into* ⅛*-inch-wide strips*
1 *tablespoon* wasabi *(Japanese green horseradish powder), mixed with cold water to form a smooth, thick paste*

For the dipping sauce, bring the water and bonito flakes to a boil in a small saucepan. Reduce the heat and simmer, skimming the foam from the surface, for about 2 minutes. Pour the liquid through a strainer lined with cheesecloth. Return the liquid to the pan over moderate heat. Add the soy sauce, *mirin*, and sugar; when the liquid begins to simmer, remove from heat. Let cool to room temperature, then chill in refrigerator.

Fill a large saucepan with water and bring to a boil. Add the *soba* and cook until al dente. Thoroughly drain, rinsing under cold running water until cool. Drain well again.

Mound the noodles in four individual serving bowls and top with tofu cubes and strips of *nori*. Place small mounds of *wasabi* paste on the side of individual shallow sauce bowls beside each serving. Pass the chilled dipping sauce for guests to season to taste with the *wasabi* for dipping or pouring over the noodles.

MAKES 4 SERVINGS

Cold Soba with Pickled Vegetables

JAPAN

The quickly pickled mixture of fresh vegetables provides a contrast of bright color, tangy flavor, and crisp texture to the cool buckwheat noodles. The dish's dipping sauce gains multidimensional flavor from syrupy *mirin* cooking wine and rich dried bonito flakes, and other vivid contrasts are provided by the spicy-hot Japanese horseradish known as *wasabi* and by meaty *shiitake* mushrooms; all may be found in Japanese markets or well-stocked food stores.

1½ cups cold water
¼ cup dried bonito flakes
½ cup light soy sauce
½ cup mirin (Japanese rice wine)
2 tablespoons sugar
½ cup coarsely shredded daikon (Japanese white radish)
½ cup coarsely shredded carrot
½ cup thinly sliced broccoli florets
6 dried shiitake mushrooms, soaked in warm water until soft, rinsed well, stems trimmed off and discarded, caps chopped coarse
1 tablespoon salt
1 pound dried soba (Japanese buckwheat noodles)
1½ tablespoons rice vinegar
1 tablespoon wasabi (Japanese green horseradish powder), mixed with cold water to form a smooth, thick paste

Bring half of the water and the bonito flakes to a boil in a small saucepan. Reduce the heat and simmer, skimming the foam from the surface, for about 2 minutes. Pour the liquid through a strainer lined with cheesecloth and return the liquid to the pan over moderate heat. Add the soy sauce, *mirin*, and half of the sugar; when the liquid begins to simmer, remove it from the heat. Let cool to room temperature, then chill in the refrigerator.

Meanwhile, in a mixing bowl, toss together the daikon, carrot, broccoli, mushrooms, and salt; add the remaining water and leave at room temperature 30 minutes to 1 hour.

Bring a large saucepan of water to a boil, add the *soba* and cook until al dente. Thoroughly drain; then rinse under cold running water until cool and drain well once again. Set aside.

Thoroughly drain the salted vegetables, squeezing them dry in your hands. Rinse out and dry the bowl, return the vegetables to it, and toss well with the rice vinegar and remaining sugar.

Mound the reserved noodles in the centers of four individual serving bowls. Arrange the pickled vegetable mixture on top. Place small mounds of *wasabi* paste on the side of individual shallow sauce bowls beside each serving. Pass the chilled dipping sauce for guests to season to taste with the *wasabi* for dipping or pouring over the noodles.

MAKES 4 SERVINGS

Cold Soba with Grated Daikon Radish

JAPAN

Grated Japanese white radish, daikon, and shreds of the sweet-hot pickled ginger familiar from sushi bars, together add a refreshing edge to this noodle dish when stirred into its dipping sauce.

> 1 pound dried soba (Japanese buckwheat
>   noodles)
> ¾ cup light soy sauce
> ¾ cup rice vinegar
> ⅓ cup grated fresh daikon (Japanese
>   white radish)
> ¼ cup thinly sliced scallions
> 2 tablespoons pickled pink ginger slices,
>   cut crosswise into thin shreds
> 12 ice cubes

Fill a large saucepan with water and bring to a boil. Add the *soba* and cook until al dente. Thoroughly drain, rinsing under cold running water until cool and draining well once again.

In a mixing bowl, stir together the soy sauce, rice vinegar, and daikon.

Mound the noodles in four individual serving bowls and pour the sauce over them. Garnish with sliced scallions and pink ginger shreds. Place 3 ice cubes on top of each mound.

MAKES 4 SERVINGS

Cold Soba with Tempura Crisps

JAPAN

Crisp, light little wisps of tempura batter provide a surprising contrast to cold buckwheat noodles. They also may be sprinkled over hot noodles with broth.

½ egg yolk
¾ cup cold water
¾ cup all-purpose flour
Vegetable oil for deep frying
1 pound dried soba (Japanese buckwheat
  noodles)
¾ cup light soy sauce
¾ cup rice vinegar
1½ tablespoons grated fresh gingerroot
2 tablespoons thinly sliced scallions

In a mixing bowl, briskly stir together the egg yolk and cold water. Put the flour in a sifter or wire sieve and sift it into the bowl. Stir just until the ingredients combine to make a thin batter; do not overstir.

Heat 1 to 2 inches of oil in a heavy skillet over moderate heat until it reaches 350°F on a deep-frying thermometer. With a spoon, drizzle the batter into the oil to form thin wisps, taking care not to crowd the skillet; fry until they are golden, 2 to 3 minutes. Remove with a wire skimmer and drain on paper towels. Repeat with remaining batter.

Fill a large saucepan with water and bring to a boil. Add the *soba* and cook until al dente. Thoroughly drain, rinsing under cold running water until cool and draining well once again.

In a mixing bowl, stir together the soy sauce, vinegar, and ginger.

Mound the noodles in four individual serving bowls; pour the sauce over them. Scatter the tempura crisps generously on top and garnish with scallions.

MAKES 4 SERVINGS

Soba Salad with Smoked Ham and Vegetables

JAPAN

Traditionally, these noodles are served on bamboo mats, accompanied by a dipping sauce redolent with the flavors of rich bonito flakes and sweet *mirin*—both available in Japanese markets and well-stocked supermarkets. Stir the spicy-hot mustard and the scallions into the dipping sauce to taste before dipping the noodles into the sauce.

¾ cup water
¼ cup dried bonito flakes
½ cup light soy sauce
½ cup mirin (Japanese rice wine)
1 tablespoon sugar
1 pound dried soba (Japanese buckwheat noodles)
¾ pound asparagus, cut diagonally into thin slices

1 pound precooked smoked ham, cut into thin strips
2 Roma tomatoes, cut into thin wedges
2 medium-sized scallions, sliced thin
1½ tablespoons hot mustard powder, mixed with cold water to form a smooth, thick paste

For the dipping sauce, bring the water and bonito flakes to a boil in a small saucepan. Reduce heat and simmer, skimming the foam from the surface, for about 2 minutes. Pour the liquid through a cheesecloth-lined strainer and return the liquid to the pan over moderate heat. Add the soy sauce, *mirin*, and sugar; when the liquid begins to simmer, remove it from heat. Let cool to room temperature, then chill in refrigerator.

Fill a large saucepan and a medium saucepan with water and bring both to a boil. Add the *soba* to the large pan and cook until al dente; add the asparagus to the small pan and cook until tender-crisp. Thoroughly drain both the noodles and the asparagus, rinsing under cold running water until cool and draining well once again.

Toss together the noodles and asparagus. Mound them in the centers of four individual serving plates. Scatter the ham on top. Garnish with tomato wedges and a few scallions. Place small mounds of mustard paste and scallions beside the noodles on each serving. Pour the chilled dipping sauce into small bowls to serve with the noodles.

MAKES 4 SERVINGS

Curried Chicken on a Bed of Soba

Buckwheat noodles provide a flavorful foil to the mild spiciness of a light, rapidly sautéed chicken breast curry.

2 tablespoons vegetable oil	3 tablespoons mild curry powder
2 tablespoons unsalted butter	2 tablespoons grated fresh gingerroot
1½ pounds boneless skinless chicken breasts, trimmed and cut into ¾-inch chunks	1 tablespoon sugar
	1 cup chicken broth
	2 tablespoons rice vinegar
1 medium-sized onion, cut into ½-inch pieces	1 pound dried soba (Japanese buckwheat noodles)
1 small green bell pepper, halved, stemmed, seeded, and cut into ½-inch squares	½ cup whipping cream
	Salt and white pepper
	¼ cup thinly sliced scallions

In a large skillet, heat 1 tablespoon each of the oil and the butter over moderately high heat. Add the chicken pieces and sauté until lightly browned on all sides, 5 to 7 minutes. Remove from the skillet and set aside.

Heat remaining oil and butter in skillet. Add the onion and bell pepper and sauté until onion is translucent, 3 to 5 minutes. Add the curry powder, ginger, and sugar and sauté 1 minute. Add the broth and rice vinegar and stir and scrape to dissolve the pan deposits. Bring liquid to a boil, reduce heat, add the reserved chicken, and simmer gently until liquid has reduced by about half and the chicken is done, about 15 minutes.

Meanwhile, fill a large saucepan with water and bring to a boil. Add the soba and cook until al dente. Drain well.

Add the cream to the curry and continue simmering until the sauce is thick. Season to taste with salt and white pepper.

Arrange the noodles on four individual serving plates and spoon the chicken and sauce on top. Garnish with scallions.

MAKES 4 SERVINGS

Cold Buckwheat Noodles with Beef and Chili

KOREA

This variation on the Korean bean-thread dish Cold Bean Threads in Chili Sauce with Braised Beef (see Index) is more robustly seasoned to stand up to the stronger flavor of buckwheat noodles.

1 pound beef flank steak
1 quart beef stock
½ cup light soy sauce
¼ cup mirin (Japanese rice wine)
1 tablespoon brown sugar
¼ teaspoon whole black peppercorns
4 (¼-inch-thick) slices fresh gingerroot
6 medium-sized garlic cloves, peeled
2 small hot red or green fresh chilies,
    halved lengthwise
1 pound dried Korean buckwheat noodles
    or Japanese soba
¼ cup Asian hot chili sauce
¼ cup marinade liquid drained from
    bottled kimchee cabbage
1 tablespoon Asian chili-sesame oil
1 cup bottled kimchee cabbage, drained
2 hard-boiled eggs, sliced thin
1 cup daikon sprouts
2 medium-sized scallions, sliced thin

Put the beef in a medium saucepan with the stock, 6 tablespoons of the soy sauce, the *mirin*, sugar, peppercorns, ginger, garlic, and chilies. Bring to a boil over moderate heat, skimming the foam that rises to the surface; reduce the heat to low, cover, and simmer gently until the meat is very tender, 2 to 2½ hours. Remove from the heat and let cool to room temperature; then transfer the beef and liquid to a bowl, cover with plastic wrap, and refrigerate until cold, about 2 hours.

Before serving, fill a large saucepan with water and bring to a boil. Add the buckwheat noodles and cook until al dente. Thoroughly drain, rinsing under cold running water until cool and draining well once again.

In another bowl, stir together the chili sauce, kimchee liquid, and chili-sesame oil with ¼ cup of the chilled braising liquid from the beef. Add the noodles and toss well to coat them. Set aside.

With a sharp knife, cut the beef across the grain into ⅛- to ¼-inch-thick slices.

Mound the reserved noodles in four large individual serving bowls. Drape the beef on top and garnish with the kimchee, eggs, daikon sprouts, and scallions.

MAKES 4 SERVINGS

Stir-Fried Soba with Beef

JAPAN

This quick stir-fry resembles Chinese *lo mein*. Substitute chicken for the beef, if you wish.

1 pound dried soba (Japanese buckwheat
  noodles)
⅓ cup peanut or vegetable oil
1 medium-sized garlic clove, chopped fine
1 tablespoon grated fresh gingerroot
1 medium-sized onion, halved and sliced thin
¾ pound beef flank steak, cut crosswise
  into ¼-inch-thick slices
4 medium-sized scallions, cut into 1-inch shreds
¼ cup chicken broth
¼ cup light soy sauce
1 tablespoon dry sherry
1 tablespoon sugar
½ teaspoon salt

Bring a large pan of water to a boil, add the *soba*, and cook until al dente. Drain well, transfer to a bowl, and toss with 2 tablespoons of the oil until well coated. Set aside.

In a large wok or skillet, heat 2 tablespoons more of the oil over moderately high heat. Add the garlic and ginger; as soon as they sizzle, add the onion and stir-fry about 1 minute. Add the beef and scallions and stir-fry until the beef begins to brown, 3 to 5 minutes. Remove from the wok and set aside.

Heat the remaining oil in the wok. Add the reserved noodles and let them sit until slightly browned, about 1 minute. Then return the reserved beef mixture to the wok, add the broth, soy sauce, sherry, sugar, and salt and continue stir-frying until the liquid has been almost completely absorbed or evaporated, 5 to 7 minutes.

MAKES 4 SERVINGS

4
BEAN THREADS AND OTHER VEGETABLE-BASED NOODLES

Made from starch extracted from mung beans, bean threads have a threadlike fineness and, when rehydrated, a crystal-clear transparency that inspires the many other names by which they are known: cellophane noodles, glass noodles, transparent noodles, silver noodles, and so on. They are sometimes also known simply as vermicelli, for their shape approximates the familiar Italian pasta. And, of course, they have a wide range of Asian names: *woon sen* in Thai, *foon see* or *fen szu* in Chinese, *so un* in Indonesian, and so on.

You'll find bean threads in any Asian market. Less widely available, but worth seeking out, are other kinds of noodles that, though they look very similar to bean threads and are virtually interchangeable with them, actually are made from different types of vegetable starch: Japanese potato-and-corn *harusame* or yam-starch *shirataki* and Korean potato-starch *dang myeon*.

All these clear noodles are essentially cooked as part of the manufacturing process. So they need only be briefly soaked—anywhere from 5 to 20 minutes, depending on the brand and its origin—in warm water to rehydrate them before use in most recipes. The resulting texture is an intriguing combination of elasticity and tenderness. Alternatively, the dry noodles are sometimes deep-fried to a puffy, crunchy texture.

Because the noodles are typically sold in long bundles, like hanks of yarn, they must be cut by the cook into shorter, more easily eaten lengths. This is best accomplished by leaving them tied together, as they are in their package, during soaking, then using scissors to cut through the loops at the ends of the bundles. To prepare smaller pieces for deep-frying, untie the dry noodles and break them by hand inside a large paper bag, which will prevent fragments from scattering.

Spiced Chicken Soup with Bean Threads

INDONESIA

Known as *soto ayam*, this is one of myriad versions of one of Indonesia's greatest soups—a satisfying main course in a bowl. A bright-tasting array of seasonings—including refreshingly acidic lemongrass, available in Asian markets—complements the chicken and noodles.

4 medium-sized shallots, peeled
2 teaspoons grated fresh gingerroot
2 small red or green fresh chili peppers,
    stemmed
1 teaspoon ground coriander
1 teaspoon salt
1 tablespoon plus 1 teaspoon sugar
1 tablespoon vegetable oil
1 (3- to 3½-pound) whole chicken, cut
    into serving pieces
1 to 1½ quarts water
1 stalk fresh lemongrass, cut into 1-inch
    pieces, or 1 tablespoon dried
    lemongrass
6 ounces bean threads
¼ pound bean sprouts
2 tablespoons light soy sauce
2 medium-sized scallions, sliced thin
1 lemon, cut into wedges

In a food processor with the metal blade, process the shallots, ginger, chilies, coriander, salt, and 1 teaspoon of the sugar, until they form a fine paste. In a small skillet, heat the oil over moderate heat. Add the paste and sauté 1 minute. Set aside.

Put the chicken in a large saucepan and add water to cover. Bring to a boil over moderate heat, skimming off the foam that rises to the surface. When no more foam forms, stir in the reserved spice paste and the lemongrass. Reduce the heat and simmer gently, partially covered, until the chicken is tender, about 1 hour, adding a little more water if necessary to keep the chicken covered.

Meanwhile, put the noodles in a large bowl and add warm water to cover well. Leave them to soak until soft. When they are tender, drain well and use scissors to cut them into 2- to 4-inch lengths. Set aside.

At the same time, bring a small saucepan of water to a boil. Add the bean sprouts and boil about 2 minutes. Drain, rinse under cold running water, drain again, and set aside.

When the chicken is done, remove it from the pan and set the cooking broth aside. As soon as the chicken is cool enough to handle, remove and discard the skin and bones; cut the meat into bite-sized chunks.

In a small bowl, stir together the soy sauce and the remaining sugar until the sugar dissolves. Set aside.

Before serving, arrange the reserved bean threads in four large serving bowls and top with the reserved bean sprouts, chunks of chicken, and scallions. Bring the reserved spiced chicken broth back to a boil and ladle it into each bowl. Pass the reserved sweetened soy sauce and lemon wedges for each diner to season his or her individual portion to taste.

MAKES 4 SERVINGS

Silver Noodle Salad with Grilled Shrimp and Chili-Lime Dressing

THAILAND

Serve this as a refreshing luncheon salad. Try it with scallops or rings of fresh baby squid, if you wish. The briny-tasting fish sauce, hot red chili paste, and dark-brown Asian sesame oil made from toasted seeds are all available in Asian markets and in the specialty foods sections of well-stocked supermarkets.

⅓ cup lime juice

2 tablespoons Asian sesame oil

1 medium-sized garlic clove, chopped fine

¾ pound medium-sized fresh shrimp, peeled and deveined, tails left on

¾ pound bean threads

1 tablespoon sugar

1 tablespoon Asian hot chili sauce

½ tablespoon fish sauce

¼ cup peanut oil

Salt and white pepper

2 medium-sized scallions, cut into 1-inch shreds

1 red bell pepper, quartered, stemmed, seeded, quarters cut crosswise into ¼-inch-wide slices

1 medium-sized carrot, shredded coarse

1 dozen Bibb, red leaf, or romaine lettuce leaves

¼ cup coarsely chopped toasted peanuts (see Index)

2 tablespoons coarsely chopped fresh cilantro

In a mixing bowl, stir together 2 tablespoons of the lime juice and 1 tablespoon of the sesame oil with the garlic. Add the shrimp and toss well to coat. Leave to marinate at room temperature 20 to 30 minutes.

Meanwhile, put the noodles in a large bowl and add warm water to cover well. Leave them to soak until soft. When they are tender, drain well and use scissors to cut them into 2- to 4-inch lengths. Set aside.

At the same time, make the dressing by stirring together the remaining lime juice with the sugar and chili and fish sauces, then slowly stirring in the remaining sesame oil and the peanut oil; season to taste with salt and pepper.

Preheat the grill or broiler until very hot. Sprinkle the shrimp with salt and pepper and grill just until done, 1 to 1½ minutes per side.

While the shrimp are grilling, put the reserved noodles in a mixing bowl with the scallions, bell pepper, and carrot. Add enough dressing to coat them generously, tossing well.

Arrange the lettuce leaves on a serving platter or on four individual plates and mound the noodle salad in the center. Top with the shrimp and garnish with peanuts and cilantro.

MAKES 4 SERVINGS

Chap Chae

One of Korea's best-known dishes, this noodle stir-fry may be served as an appetizer, wrapped in butter lettuce or romaine leaves, or as a side dish with grilled meat, poultry, or seafood. Small, shriveled tree fungus—sometimes known as cloud ear mushrooms—are widely available in Asian markets, as is the dark, aromatic variety of sesame oil pressed from toasted seeds.

½ pound bean threads or other vegetable-starch noodles
¼ cup small dried black tree fungus
1½ tablespoons Asian sesame oil
1½ tablespoons light soy sauce
1 tablespoon sugar
¼ cup vegetable oil
2 medium-sized garlic cloves, chopped fine
4 medium-sized leaves Nappa cabbage, cut crosswise into ⅛-inch-wide shreds

2 large scallions, cut into 1- to 2-inch-long slivers
1 medium-sized carrot, cut into thin julienne strips
1 medium-sized red bell pepper, quartered, stemmed, seeded, quarters cut crosswise into ⅛-inch-wide slices
1 tablespoon black sesame seeds or toasted white sesame seeds (see Index)

Put the noodles in a large bowl and add warm water to cover well. Leave them to soak until soft. At the same time, in a separate bowl, cover the tree fungus with warm water and leave to soak until soft, about 20 minutes.

When the noodles are tender, drain well, and use scissors to cut them into 2- to 4-inch lengths. Drain the fungus, rinse well, and cut into ⅛-inch-wide strips.

In a small bowl or cup, stir together the sesame oil, soy sauce, and sugar; set aside.

In a large skillet or wok, heat the vegetable oil over moderately high heat. Add the garlic; as soon as it sizzles, add the cabbage, scallions, carrot, bell pepper, and fungus; stir-fry for 1 minute. Stir in the reserved sesame-soy mixture and then the noodles; stir briefly to mix, then transfer to a serving dish or bowl. Garnish with sesame seeds.

MAKES 4 SERVINGS

Stir-Fried Spicy String Beans
with Bean Threads

THAILAND

The slippery texture of the bean thread noodles contrasts pleasantly with the snap of the beans in this quick stir-fry, which makes an attractive, lively companion to simply cooked meat or poultry. If you want to transform this into a main course, stir-fry some thinly sliced chicken or beef, or small to medium-sized shrimp, along with the string beans. Thai red curry paste—a blend of dried red chilies, garlic, lemongrass, and other herbs and spices—may be found in Asian markets as can the aromatic, briny fish sauce.

¼ pound bean threads
2 tablespoons vegetable oil
1 medium-sized garlic clove, chopped fine
1 pound small fresh string beans,
    trimmed and cut into 2-inch lengths
1 tablespoon Thai red curry paste
1 tablespoon light soy sauce
2 teaspoons fish sauce
½ tablespoon sugar
1 tablespoon finely shredded fresh basil
    leaves

Put the noodles in a large bowl and add warm water to cover well. Leave them to soak until soft. Drain well and use scissors to cut them into 2- to 4-inch lengths. Set aside.

In a large wok or skillet, heat the oil over moderately high heat. Add the garlic; as soon as it sizzles, add the string beans and stir-fry until tender-crisp, 3 to 4 minutes.

Add the reserved noodles, curry paste, soy and fish sauces, and sugar; stir-fry 1 to 2 minutes more, until heated through and well mixed. Transfer to a serving platter and garnish with basil.

MAKES 4 SERVINGS

Stir-Fried Bean Threads with Shrimp, Onion, and Egg

THAILAND

❧

A quick, simple stir-fry ideal for lunch. This is also good with thinly sliced boneless skinless chicken breast.

¾ pound bean threads
¼ cup vegetable oil
4 medium-sized garlic cloves, chopped
fine
1 or 2 small fresh red or green hot
chilies, thinly sliced (optional)
1 medium-sized onion, halved and sliced
thin

¾ pound small to medium-sized fresh
shrimp, peeled and deveined
¼ cup fish sauce
2 tablespoons light soy sauce
2 tablespoons sugar
4 eggs, lightly beaten
2 medium-sized scallions, sliced thin
¼ cup coarsely chopped fresh cilantro

Put the noodles in a large bowl and add warm water to cover well. Leave them to soak until soft. Drain well and use scissors to cut them into 2- to 4-inch lengths.

In a large wok or skillet, heat the oil over moderately high heat. Add the garlic and, if you like, the chilies; as soon as they sizzle, add the onion and continue stir-frying until the onion just begins to turn golden, 3 to 4 minutes. Add the shrimp and stir-fry until they turn pink, about 1 minute. Add the fish and soy sauces, sugar, and noodles and continue stir-frying about 3 minutes more.

Push the contents of the wok to one side and add the eggs and scallions. As soon as the eggs begin to curdle, fold them together with the bean-thread mixture and gently stir about 1 minute more. Transfer to a platter or to four individual serving plates and garnish with cilantro.

MAKES 4 SERVINGS

Ginger Chicken Casserole with Oyster Mushrooms and Cellophane Noodles

Rich tasting and warming, this country-style dish makes an ideal winter main course. You'll find flavorful Asian sesame oil—pressed from toasted seeds—and canned oyster mushrooms in Asian markets and well-stocked supermarkets.

¾ pound bean threads

¼ cup vegetable oil

2 medium-sized scallions, chopped coarse

1 medium-sized garlic clove, chopped fine

1 tablespoon grated fresh gingerroot

1 pound boneless skinless chicken breasts
    or thighs, cut into ¾- to 1-inch chunks

½ cup chicken broth

2 tablespoons bottled oyster sauce

2 tablespoons dry sherry

½ tablespoon light soy sauce

½ tablespoon Asian sesame oil

½ tablespoon brown sugar

½ teaspoon salt

½ teaspoon white pepper

1 cup drained canned oyster mushrooms

1 tablespoon black sesame seeds or
    toasted white sesame seeds (see Index)

—93—

Put the noodles in a large bowl and add warm water to cover well. Leave them to soak until soft. Drain and use scissors to cut them into 2- to 4-inch lengths.

In a large, heavy casserole, heat half of the oil over moderately high heat. Add the scallions, garlic, and ginger; as soon as they sizzle, add the chicken and stir-fry until it loses its pink color, 2 to 3 minutes. Transfer to a bowl and set aside.

In another bowl, stir together the chicken broth, oyster sauce, sherry, soy sauce, sesame oil, sugar, salt, and pepper.

Heat the remaining oil in the casserole. Add the noodles and stir-fry about 1 minute. Add the reserved chicken, the oyster mushrooms, and the broth mixture, stir briefly to combine, reduce the heat to low, and cover. Cook gently until most of the liquid has been absorbed and the chicken is cooked through, about 15 minutes. Garnish with sesame seeds and serve from the casserole at table.

MAKES 4 SERVINGS

"Ants Climbing a Tree" with Chicken and Crispy Noodles

CHINA

This contemporized variation on the traditional Chinese dish (see Index) substitutes ground chicken for the pork and serves the savory poultry mixture atop a bed of crisply fried bean threads. Meaty *shiitake* mushrooms enhance the chicken mixture's taste and texture.

1 pound ground chicken
¼ cup light soy sauce
1 tablespoon cornstarch
2 teaspoons sugar
1 tablespoon sesame oil
1 tablespoon hot chili sauce
6 dried shiitake *mushrooms, soaked in*
    warm water until soft, rinsed well,
    stems trimmed off and discarded, caps
    chopped coarse
Vegetable oil for deep frying
½ pound bean threads, broken or cut
    into 2- to 4-inch pieces
¼ cup vegetable oil
2 medium-sized garlic cloves, chopped fine
1 tablespoon grated fresh gingerroot
1 medium to large carrot, cut into thin
    shreds
¾ cup chicken broth
2 medium to large scallions, sliced thin

Put the chicken in a mixing bowl. In a separate small bowl or cup, stir together half of the soy sauce with all of the cornstarch and sugar, until the cornstarch and sugar dissolve; stir in half each of the sesame oil and chili sauce. Stir this mixture thoroughly into the chicken and leave to marinate at room temperature about 15 minutes.

While the chicken marinates and the mushrooms soak, fry the bean threads. Preheat the oven to 200°F. In a large wok or heavy skillet, heat several inches of oil to 350°F on a deep-frying thermometer. Drop about ⅙ of the bean threads into the oil; using a wire skimmer or slotted spoon to turn them and keep them immersed, fry until they puff up uniformly, about 15 seconds. Remove to drain on paper towels, then transfer to a baking pan and keep warm in the oven. Repeat with the remaining batches of bean threads.

In a large wok or skillet, heat the ¼ cup oil over moderately high heat. Add the garlic, ginger, and carrot; as soon as they sizzle, add the marinated chicken and stir-fry until it loses its pink color, 1 to 2 minutes. Add the chicken broth, *shiitakes*, and the remaining soy and sesame oils and chili sauce; as soon as the liquid begins to simmer, reduce the heat, cover the wok, and cook until the sauce has thickened, 3 to 4 minutes more.

Arrange the crisp bean threads in a bed on a serving platter or bowl. At table, pour the chicken mixture over the center of the bean threads and garnish with scallions. Serve immediately.

MAKES 4 SERVINGS

Cold Bean Threads in Chili Sauce
with Braised Beef

KOREA

The spiciness of this cold luncheon dish is surprisingly refreshing on a hot day. Typically, the long strands of noodles are not cut before serving; if you find this too challenging, cut them with scissors into more manageable lengths after soaking. Try the recipe with dark-meat chicken, too. You'll find bottled kimchee in Asian markets, along with garlicky Asian chili sauce and rich, dark sesame oil made from toasted seeds; long, skinny, almost seedless Japanese cucumbers are becoming more widely available in good supermarkets and produce shops.

¼ cup Japanese rice vinegar
2 tablespoons plus ½ teaspoon white sugar
½ teaspoon salt
1 medium-sized Japanese cucumber, sliced paper-thin
1 pound beef flank steak
1 quart beef stock
½ cup light soy sauce
¼ cup sake (Japanese rice wine)
1 tablespoon brown sugar
¼ teaspoon whole black peppercorns
4 (¼-inch-thick) slices fresh gingerroot
4 medium-sized garlic cloves, peeled

1 pod star anise
¾ pound bean threads or other vegetable-starch noodles
¼ cup Asian hot chili sauce
¼ cup marinade liquid drained from bottled kimchee cabbage
1 tablespoon Asian sesame oil
1 cup bottled kimchee cabbage, drained
1 small daikon (Japanese white radish), sliced thin
2 eggs, hard-boiled and cut into ¼-inch slices
2 medium-sized scallions, sliced thin

In a large glass or ceramic bowl, stir together half of the rice vinegar, the ½ teaspoon of white sugar, and salt. Add the sliced cucumber, mix well, cover, and refrigerate 3 to 4 hours.

Meanwhile, put the beef in a medium saucepan with the stock, 6 tablespoons of the soy sauce, the sake, brown sugar, peppercorns, ginger, garlic, and star anise. Bring to a boil over moderate heat, skimming the foam that rises to the surface; reduce the heat to low, cover, and simmer gently until the meat is very tender, 2 to 2½ hours. Remove from the heat and let cool to room temperature, then transfer the beef and liquid to a bowl, cover with plastic wrap, and refrigerate until cold, about 2 hours.

Before serving, put the noodles in a large bowl and add warm water to cover well. Leave them to soak until soft. Drain thoroughly.

In another bowl, stir together the chili sauce, kimchee liquid, and sesame oil with the remaining rice vinegar, white sugar, soy sauce, and ¼ cup of the chilled braising liquid from the beef. Add the drained noodles and toss well to coat them. Set aside.

With a sharp knife, cut the beef across the grain into ⅛- to ¼-inch-thick slices.

Mound the reserved noodles in four large individual serving bowls. Drape the beef on top and garnish with the pickled cucumber, kimchee, sliced daikon, and eggs. Garnish with scallions.

MAKES 4 SERVINGS

Beef Sukiyaki

JAPAN

 Yam-starch *shirataki* noodles or more widely available bean threads are a significant element in this widely known Japanese specialty of beef steak quickly cooked at table in soy sauce and sake. Make it with thinly sliced boneless, skinless chicken, if you like. Serve steamed rice on the side.

> 1½ pounds beef tenderloin or sirloin
>   steak, well trimmed
> ¾ pound dried shirataki or bean threads
> ⅔ cup Japanese soy sauce
> ⅔ cup sake (Japanese rice wine)
> ⅓ cup sugar
> 2 medium-sized onions, cut into ¼-inch-
>   thick slices
> 1 cup thinly sliced canned bamboo
>   shoots
> ¼ pound cultivated mushrooms, cut into
>   ¼-inch-thick slices
> 4 medium-sized scallions, cut into 1- to
>   2-inch lengths
> 2 medium-sized carrots, sliced thin
> ½ pound firm Chinese-style tofu,
>   drained well and cut into ½- to ¾-inch
>   cubes
> ¼ cup vegetable oil
> 6 cups steamed white rice

 Wrap the beef in plastic wrap and put it in the freezer until it firms up, 30 to 45 minutes. Put the noodles in a large bowl and add warm water to cover well. Leave them to soak until soft.

Cut the beef crosswise into tissue-thin slices. Drain the noodles and use scissors to cut them into 2- to 4-inch lengths.

In a mixing bowl, stir together the soy sauce, sake, and sugar until the sugar dissolves. Set aside.

Arrange the beef, noodles, onions, bamboo shoots, mushrooms, scallions, carrots, and tofu attractively on a serving platter.

At the dining table, in a large electric skillet, heat a little of the oil over moderately high heat. Drape slices of beef evenly over the bottom of the pan, sprinkle lightly with the reserved soy mixture, and sauté, turning with long chopsticks or a long fork, until cooked through, about 1 minute per side. Push the meat to one side of the skillet, pour in a little more oil, and spread some of the noodles, vegetables, and tofu, sprinkling with the sauce; sauté 1 to 2 minutes more. Push to one side and continue cooking the meat, noodles, and vegetables, adding progressively more of the sauce so that all the ingredients simmer in the liquid.

As the meat and vegetables are done, let guests transfer them to individual bowls of rice, spooning some of the hot liquid from the pan over each serving.

MAKES 4 SERVINGS

Chap Chae with Beef

KOREA

This main-course variation on Chap Chae (see Index) includes thin strips of marinated beef, whose chewiness—along with that of the *shiitake* mushrooms—contrasts pleasantly with the slippery noodles. Asian sesame oil, made from toasted sesame seeds, adds rich flavor and texture; you'll find it, along with other special ingredients, in Asian food shops or well-stocked supermarkets.

¾ *pound lean beef steak, well trimmed*
¼ *pound bean threads or other vegetable-*
 starch noodles
6 *dried* shiitake *mushrooms*
1 *tablespoon grated fresh gingerroot*
1 *tablespoon rice wine vinegar*
2 *tablespoons Asian sesame oil*
2 *tablespoons light soy sauce*
2 *teaspoons sugar*
¼ *cup vegetable oil*
2 *medium-sized garlic cloves, chopped*
 fine
½ *to 1 teaspoon crushed red chili flakes*
1 *medium-sized onion, halved and sliced*
 thin
1 *medium-sized carrot, cut into thin*
 julienne strips
1 *small to medium-sized daikon*
 (Japanese white radish), cut into
 julienne strips
1 *medium-sized green bell pepper,*
 quartered, stemmed, seeded, quarters
 cut crosswise into ⅛-inch-wide slices
1 *tablespoon black sesame seeds or*
 toasted white sesame seeds (see Index)

Wrap the beef in plastic wrap and put it in the freezer until it firms up, about 30 minutes. Put the noodles in a large bowl and add warm water to cover well. Leave them to soak until soft. At the same time, in another bowl, cover the mushrooms with warm water and leave to soak until soft, about 20 minutes.

Cut the beef crosswise into thin slices. Then cut the slices lengthwise into thin strips. In a bowl, toss the strips together with the ginger, rice wine vinegar, and half each of the sesame oil and soy sauce. Leave to marinate at room temperature 10 to 15 minutes.

Drain the noodles and use scissors to cut them into 2- to 4-inch lengths. Drain the mushrooms, rinse well, trim off and discard their stems, and cut their caps into $\frac{1}{8}$-inch-wide strips.

In a small bowl or cup, stir together the remaining sesame oil and soy sauce with the sugar; set aside.

In a large skillet or wok, heat half of the vegetable oil over moderately high heat. Add the garlic and crushed pepper; as soon as they sizzle, add the onion, carrot, daikon, bell pepper, and mushrooms. Stir-fry for 1 minute. Remove from the skillet and set aside.

Heat the remaining oil, add the beef, and stir-fry until evenly browned, 2 to 3 minutes. Stir in the reserved sesame-soy mixture, the reserved vegetables, and the noodles; stir briefly to mix, then transfer to a serving dish or bowl. Garnish with sesame seeds.

MAKES 4 SERVINGS

Stir-Fried Silver Noodles with Pork, Tomato, and Chilies

THAILAND

If you'd prefer, make this sweet-spicy dish with beef, chicken, or shrimp instead of pork. The fish sauce, available in Asian markets or well-stocked supermarkets, adds a pleasantly briny undertone.

½ pound bean threads
¼ cup vegetable oil
2 medium-sized garlic cloves, chopped fine
2 small red or green chili peppers, halved lengthwise, stemmed, seeded, and chopped fine
1 medium-sized scallion, cut into 1-inch shreds
½ tablespoon grated fresh gingerroot

¾ pound pork tenderloin, well trimmed and cut crosswise into ¼-inch-thick slices
6 medium-sized Roma tomatoes, cored and chopped coarse
1½ tablespoons fish sauce
1½ tablespoons light soy sauce
2 teaspoons brown sugar
2 tablespoons coarsely chopped fresh cilantro

Put the noodles in a large bowl and add warm water to cover well. Leave them to soak until soft. Drain well and use scissors to cut them into 2- to 4-inch lengths.

In a large wok or skillet, heat the oil over moderately high heat. Add the garlic, chilies, scallion, and ginger; as soon as they sizzle, add the pork and stir-fry until it loses its pink color, 2 to 3 minutes.

Stir in the tomatoes, fish and soy sauces, and sugar. As soon as the liquid begins to simmer, add the noodles and stir-fry gently to mix the ingredients well. Transfer to a platter or to four individual plates and garnish with cilantro.

MAKES 4 SERVINGS

Stir-Fried Bean Threads with Sweet Sausage and Vegetables

This reinterpretation of Cantonese chow mein, made with clear bean threads, features sweet, anise-flavored Chinese cured sausage, available in Asian markets. The fish sauce, available in Asian markets and the specialty food aisles of well-stocked supermarkets, adds a subtle briny contrast. For a more elaborate version, add some thinly sliced chicken and small to medium-sized fresh shrimp.

½ pound bean threads
¼ cup vegetable oil
2 medium-sized garlic cloves, chopped fine
1 tablespoon grated fresh gingerroot
½ pound Chinese sausage, cut diagonally into ¼-inch-thick slices
4 medium-sized leaves Nappa cabbage, cut crosswise into ¼-inch-wide shreds

1 small onion, halved and sliced thin
1 medium-sized carrot, cut into ¼-inch-wide shreds
¾ cup chicken broth
1 tablespoon fish sauce
2 teaspoons light soy sauce
2 medium-sized scallions, sliced thin
1 lemon, cut into wedges

—103—

Put the noodles in a large bowl and add warm water to cover well. Leave them to soak until soft. Drain well and use scissors to cut them into 2- to 4-inch lengths.

In a large wok or skillet, heat half of the oil over moderate heat. Add the noodles and stir-fry until they begin to brown, 3 to 4 minutes. Remove from the wok and set aside.

Heat the remaining oil in the wok over moderately high heat. Add the garlic and ginger; as soon as they sizzle, add the sausage and stir-fry 1 to 2 minutes. Add the cabbage, onion, and carrot and stir-fry 3 to 4 minutes more.

Add the broth, fish sauce, soy sauce, and the reserved noodles. Stir-fry until the ingredients are well mixed and most of the liquid has evaporated or been absorbed by the noodles, 2 to 3 minutes more. Transfer to a platter or to four individual plates, garnish with scallions, and serve with lemon wedges to be squeezed over the noodles to taste.

MAKES 4 SERVINGS

Traditional "Ants Climbing a Tree"

CHINA

The fanciful name is meant to describe the tiny bits of ground pork scattered in the sauce atop a "bark" of bean thread noodles.

½ pound bean threads
1 pound lean ground pork
¼ cup light soy sauce
2 teaspoons cornstarch
2 teaspoons sugar
1 tablespoon sesame oil
1 tablespoon hot chili sauce
¼ cup vegetable oil
2 medium to large scallions, sliced thin
2 medium-sized garlic cloves, chopped fine
1 tablespoon grated fresh gingerroot
1 cup chicken broth

Put the noodles in a large bowl and add warm water to cover well. Leave them to soak until soft and use scissors to cut them into 6- to 8-inch strands. Drain thoroughly.

Meanwhile, put the pork in a mixing bowl. In a separate small bowl or cup, stir together half of the soy sauce with all of the cornstarch and sugar, until the cornstarch and sugar dissolve; stir in half each of the sesame oil and chili sauce. Stir this mixture thoroughly into the pork and leave to marinate at room temperature about 15 minutes.

In a large wok or skillet, heat oil over moderately high heat. Add the scallions, garlic, and ginger; as soon as they sizzle, add the marinated pork and stir-fry until it loses its pink color, 1 to 2 minutes. Add the chicken broth, remaining soy and sesame oils, and chili sauce; as soon as the liquid begins to simmer, add the noodles, stirring well. Reduce heat, cover, and cook just until the liquid has thickened and most of it has been absorbed by the noodles, 3 to 4 minutes more. Stir briefly and transfer to a serving platter.

MAKES 4 SERVINGS

5
R ICE STICKS

Noodles made from cooked rice are prevalent throughout Southeast Asia and also can be found in the cuisines of China and Japan. Tender, mildly sweet in flavor, and pale in color, they make an excellent foil for both subtle and vibrantly spiced toppings.

Rice noodles are most commonly available in dried forms and are sold in Asian markets and the specialty food sections of good-sized supermarkets. Their size varies from thin wisps of rice vermicelli to ribbons resembling linguine and fettucine to spaghetti-like strands. Names vary with the country of origin—including Chinese *mee fun,* Thai *sen mee,* Malaysian *laksa,* Philippine *lug-lug,* and Vietnamese *banh-pho*—and shapes and packaging likewise will differ depending on the source. In the recipes that follow, I've tried to specify appropriate shapes to seek, but you should feel free to substitute whatever similar form is available to you. Fresh rice noodles also can be found in the refrigerated case of Asian markets, and while a few of the following recipes call for them, you can substitute dried noodles if necessary.

Because they already have been cooked as part of the manufacturing process, the preparation of rice noodles is fairly simple. Dried noodles require only soaking to rehydrate them before they are added to the wok or topped with other ingredients. Fresh noodles generally require only a rinsing with boiling water to remove the oil coating that prevents them from sticking together; brief cooking safeguards their tender texture.

Pho Noodle Soup with Beef Sirloin, Mint, and Basil

VIETNAM

Throughout Vietnam, and in Vietnamese enclaves the world over, fragrant bowls of soup and rice noodles—topped with a wide variety of meats—are dished up at breakfast and lunch in cafés known as *pho* shops, after the type of noodles used. The fish sauce, a favorite Southeast Asian seasoning, adds a subtle briny flavor. Serve bottled Asian chili sauce on the side, for each guest to spice up his or her serving. Both condiments are available in Asian markets and well-stocked supermarkets.

¾ pound good-quality lean boneless beef
sirloin, well trimmed
½ pound wide dried rice sticks or ¾
pound fresh rice sticks
1 quart beef broth
1 quart chicken broth
3 (¼-inch-thick) slices fresh gingerroot
2 whole pods star anise
1 cinnamon stick
½ small onion, sliced thin
2 cups bean sprouts
2 small fresh red or green chilies, cut
crosswise into thin slices
¼ cup packed fresh basil leaves
¼ cup packed fresh mint leaves
1 tablespoon fish sauce
2 limes, cut into wedges
Hot chili sauce

Wrap the steak in plastic wrap and put in the freezer to chill until fairly firm, 30 to 45 minutes.

If using dried rice noodles, put them in a large bowl and add cold water to cover well. Leave them to soak until soft, about 30 minutes.

As soon as the beef starts chilling and the noodles start soaking, put the beef and chicken broths, ginger, star anise, cinnamon, and onion in a saucepan. Bring to a boil, reduce the heat, and simmer gently, covered, about 30 minutes. With a slotted spoon, remove and discard the ginger, star anise, cinnamon, and onion. Set aside.

If using fresh rice noodles, put them in a colander or strainer. Bring a pot or kettle of water to a boil and pour over the noodles to rinse, soften, and warm them.

Drain the fresh or dried soaked noodles thoroughly and mound them in four large deep serving bowls. On a serving platter, arrange mounds of bean sprouts, chilies, basil, and mint.

With a very sharp knife, cut the beef across the grain into the thinnest slices possible. Drape the slices over the noodles in each bowl.

Bring the reserved broth back to a boil and season to taste with fish sauce. Ladle the boiling broth over the beef and noodles; the heat of the broth will cook the meat. Serve immediately, letting each guest garnish and season his or her serving to taste with bean sprouts, herbs, squeezes of lime, and chili sauce.

MAKES 4 SERVINGS

Lemongrass Soup with Rice Sticks and Chicken

THAILAND

A quick and inexpensive way to use up leftover roast chicken, this recipe is a Thai lunchtime favorite, its lively flavor resulting from a combination of citrusy lemongrass and briny fish sauce—both available in Asian markets and well-stocked supermarkets.

> ¾ pound fresh broad rice sticks or ½
>   pound dried broad rice sticks
> 6 cups chicken broth
> 2 stalks fresh lemongrass, cut into 2-inch
>   pieces, or 2 long strips lemon zest
> 2 cups cooked chicken meat, torn into
>   thin shreds
> ¼ cup fish sauce
> 2 tablespoons hot chili oil (optional)
> 2 medium-sized scallions, sliced thin
> ¼ cup coarsely chopped fresh cilantro
> 1 lime, cut into wedges

If using fresh rice noodles, put them in a colander or strainer. Bring a pan or kettle of water to a boil and pour over the noodles to rinse, soften, and warm them. If using dried rice noodles, put them in a large bowl and add cold water to cover well. Leave them to soak until soft, about 30 minutes. Drain the noodles thoroughly.

Put the broth and lemongrass in a saucepan and bring to a boil over moderate heat. Reduce the heat, cover, and simmer about 5 minutes.

Mound the noodles in four individual serving bowls. Scatter the chicken over the noodles and sprinkle with the fish sauce and chili oil to taste. Ladle the hot broth into each bowl and float scallions and cilantro on top. Serve with lime wedges for each guest to squeeze in to taste.

MAKES 4 SERVINGS

Rice Stick Salad with Bay Shrimp and Vegetables

JAPAN

The key to this quickly prepared salad lies in cutting up the ingredients to a fineness that complements the thin rice noodles. Of course, the pale, slender *enoki* mushrooms—sold fresh in Asian markets and well-stocked supermarkets and produce shops—need no cutting. If you like, add some slivers of smoked ham to the mixture. The Asian sesame oil, pressed from toasted seeds, adds extra richness.

10 ounces thin rice vermicelli, roughly broken into 1- to 2-inch pieces
¼ cup rice vinegar
2 tablespoons lemon juice
1 tablespoon finely chopped crystallized ginger
1 teaspoon light soy sauce
½ cup vegetable oil
2 teaspoons Asian sesame oil
¾ pound cooked bay shrimp
¼ pound fresh daikon sprouts

3 to 4 ounces fresh enoki *mushrooms, trimmed*
1 medium-sized red bell pepper, quartered, stemmed, seeded, quarters cut crosswise into ⅛-inch-thick slivers
1 medium-sized celery stalk, cut crosswise into ⅛-inch-thick slices
1 large scallion, cut into 1-inch shreds
Red leaf lettuce leaves
2 tablespoons toasted sesame seeds (see Index)

—109—

Put the rice sticks in a large bowl and add cold water to cover well. Leave them to soak until soft, about 30 minutes. Drain well.

While the noodles soak, stir together the rice vinegar, lemon juice, crystallized ginger, and soy sauce. Stirring continuously with a small whisk or a fork, stir in the vegetable and sesame oils. Set this dressing aside.

In a mixing bowl, toss together the noodles with the shrimp, daikon sprouts, mushrooms, bell pepper, celery, and scallion, adding enough of the reserved dressing to coat the ingredients evenly. Arrange the lettuce leaves on a large serving platter or on four individual plates and mound the salad on top. Garnish with sesame seeds.

MAKES 4 SERVINGS

Chinese Chicken Salad on a Bed of Crisp Rice Sticks

❧

Deep-fried thin rice sticks provide a crunchy background for this variation on a contemporary Chinese-style salad popular in the West. Slivers of *shiitake* mushrooms make the salad extra luxurious. The Asian sesame oil, pressed from toasted seeds, adds a distinctively rich flavor to the dressing.

Vegetable oil for deep frying
6 ounces thin rice vermicelli
1 small head Nappa cabbage, leaves separated, trimmed, and cut crosswise into ¼-inch strips
3 cups coarsely chopped cooked chicken
1½ cups small snow pea pods, simmered in boiling water until tender-crisp, rinsed under cold water and drained
1 cup canned mandarin orange segments, rinsed and drained
½ cup slivered almonds, toasted (see Index)

4 large dried shiitake mushrooms, soaked in warm water for 15 minutes, rinsed and drained, stems cut off and discarded, caps cut into ¼-inch-wide slices
2 medium-sized scallions, sliced thin
2 tablespoons coarsely chopped fresh cilantro leaves
¼ cup lemon juice
1 tablespoon honey
2 teaspoons light soy sauce
½ cup peanut oil
1½ tablespoons Asian sesame oil

In a large wok or heavy skillet, heat several inches of oil to 350°F on a deep-frying thermometer. Drop about ⅙ of the noodles into the oil; using a wire skimmer or slotted spoon to turn them and keep them immersed, fry until they puff up uniformly, about 15 seconds. Remove to drain on paper towels. Repeat with the remaining batches of noodles.

In a large salad bowl or serving bowl, preferably glass, arrange a bed of Nappa cabbage. Arrange the crisp noodles evenly on top, gently breaking them up into shorter strands.

In a mixing bowl, toss together the chicken, snow peas, mandarin oranges, almonds, mushrooms, and scallions. Mound the mixture in the center of the bed of noodles. Garnish with cilantro.

In a separate bowl, stir together the lemon juice, honey, and soy sauce until the honey has dissolved completely. Stirring continuously with a small whisk or fork, pour in the peanut and sesame oils.

Just before serving, drizzle the salad with dressing to taste, tossing all the ingredients together and adding more dressing if necessary to coat the salad evenly. Serve immediately.

MAKES 4 SERVINGS

Vegetarian Pað Thai with Crisp Tofu

THAILAND

While the presence of the fish sauce—a popular, briny condiment available in Asian markets—keeps this noodle dish from being strictly vegetarian, most people avoiding meat will find it suits them just fine.

½ pound narrow dried rice sticks
1 cup vegetable oil
½ pound firm Chinese-style tofu,
    drained well on paper towels and cut
    into ½-inch cubes
3 tablespoons cider vinegar
3 tablespoons sugar
¼ cup fish sauce
2 tablespoons tomato paste
3 medium-sized garlic cloves, chopped fine
1 fresh green chili pepper, stemmed,
    seeded, and finely chopped
1 cup small broccoli florets
1 cup carrots cut diagonally into ¼-inch-
    thick slices
2 teaspoons paprika
1 (15-ounce) can straw mushrooms, drained
1 egg, lightly beaten
Romaine or butter lettuce leaves
1 cup bean sprouts
⅓ cup toasted unsalted peanuts, chopped
    coarse (see Index)
1 medium scallion, cut into 1-inch shreds
¼ cup small fresh cilantro sprigs
1 small lime, cut into wedges

Put the rice sticks in a large bowl and add cold water to cover well. Leave them to soak until soft, about 30 minutes.

While the noodles soak, heat the oil over moderately high heat in a large wok or skillet. Add a handful of tofu cubes and fry, turning with a wire skimmer or slotted spoon, until golden brown, about 6 minutes; remove with the skimmer or spoon to drain on paper towels and repeat with remaining batches.

In a small bowl, stir together the vinegar and sugar until the sugar dissolves. Stir in the fish sauce and tomato paste and set this seasoning mixture aside.

Carefully pour off all but a few tablespoons of the oil from the wok or skillet. Over moderately high heat, add the garlic and chili; as soon as they sizzle, add the broccoli and carrots; stir-fry until their colors brighten and they begin to turn slightly golden at their edges, 3 to 4 minutes. Add the reserved seasoning mixture and sprinkle in the paprika; stir-fry about 1 minute more. Then add the drained noodles and straw mushrooms, stirring and turning the mixture until most of the liquid has been absorbed by the noodles. Add the egg and stir and turn the noodles gently until it sets, forming small, soft curds.

Line a serving bowl or platter with the lettuce leaves and mound the noodles in the center, arranging the tofu cubes on top. Scatter the bean sprouts around the mound. Sprinkle the noodles and tofu with peanuts, scallion, and cilantro. Arrange lime wedges around the sides, to be squeezed over individual portions.

MAKES 4 SERVINGS

Rice Sticks with Crab, Garlic, and Green Chilies

THAILAND

❦

Intensely garlicky, this quick noodle dish is a type of crab *pad thai*. The briny fish sauce, available in Asian markets, subtly complements the crab's flavor.

½ pound narrow dried rice sticks
2 tablespoons fish sauce
1 tablespoon sugar
1 tablespoon light soy sauce
3 tablespoons vegetable oil
6 medium-sized garlic cloves, chopped
  fine
2 small fresh green or red chilies, cut
  crosswise into very thin slices
¾ pound fresh cooked crabmeat, flaked
  coarse

2 tablespoons unsalted butter
2 eggs, lightly beaten
2 medium-sized scallions, cut into 1-inch
  shreds
Romaine or butter lettuce leaves
2 medium-sized, firm, ripe tomatoes,
  cored and cut into thin wedges
1 small cucumber, peeled and sliced thin
¼ cup small fresh cilantro sprigs
1 small lime, cut into wedges

Put the rice sticks in a large bowl and add cold water to cover well. Leave them to soak until soft, about 30 minutes. Drain well and set aside.

Meanwhile, in a separate bowl, stir together the fish sauce, sugar, and soy sauce. Set this seasoning mixture aside.

In a large wok or skillet, heat the oil over moderately high heat. Add the garlic and chilies; as soon as they sizzle, add the crab and stir-fry about 30 seconds. Add the reserved seasoning mixture and the butter, then add the drained noodles; stir and turn the mixture until most of the liquid has been absorbed by the noodles. Add the eggs and scallions and stir and turn the noodles gently until the eggs set, forming small, soft curds.

Line a serving bowl or platter with the lettuce leaves and mound the noodles in the center. Garnish with tomatoes and cucumber and sprinkle with cilantro. Arrange lime wedges around the sides, to be squeezed over individual portions.

MAKES 4 SERVINGS

Spicy Singapore Noodles with Squid

SINGAPORE

You can make this dish hotter or milder by adding more or less chili paste. Any good quality fishmonger will clean the squid for you. The rich-tasting Asian sesame oil, pressed from toasted seeds, may be found in Asian markets or well-stocked food stores.

10 ounces thin rice vermicelli
2 tablespoons light soy sauce
1 to 2 teaspoons hot chili paste
1 teaspoon Asian sesame oil
¼ cup vegetable oil
2 medium-sized garlic cloves, chopped fine
1 small onion, sliced thin
1 medium-sized scallion, cut into 1-inch shreds
2 teaspoons grated fresh gingerroot
¾ pound small squid, cleaned, body cut
   into ¼-inch-wide rings, tentacles cut
   into small clusters
1 cup bean sprouts
2 tablespoons finely chopped fresh
   cilantro leaves

Put the rice noodles in a large bowl and add cold water to cover well. Leave them to soak until soft, about 30 minutes. Drain well and set aside.

Stir together the soy sauce, chili paste, and sesame oil and set aside.

In a large wok or skillet, heat the oil over moderately high heat. Add the garlic, onion, scallion, and ginger; as soon as they sizzle, add the squid and stir-fry about 1 minute. Add the drained noodles and the bean sprouts and stir-fry about 1 minute more.

Add the reserved soy-sauce mixture and stir-fry until most of the liquid has been absorbed, about 1 minute more. Transfer to a platter and garnish with cilantro.

MAKES 4 SERVINGS

Fresh Spring Rolls Filled with Bay Shrimp and Rice Sticks

VIETNAM

A refreshing, light alternative to the familiar deep-fried Chinese spring rolls, these traditional Vietnamese appetizers enfold thick rice vermicelli, poached shrimp, vegetables, and herbs in thin rice paper wrappers available in Asian markets. Thin strips of cold poached pork also can be used along with or in place of the shrimp.

2 ounces thin rice vermicelli
12 dried rice paper wrappers
12 small butter lettuce leaves, stem ends cut out
¾ pound cooked bay shrimp
1 medium-sized carrot, shredded fine
¼ cup coarsely chopped fresh mint leaves
¼ cup coarsely shredded fresh basil leaves
Hoisin sauce (for dipping)
Hot chili sauce (for dipping)

Put the rice noodles in a large bowl and add cold water to cover well. Leave them to soak until soft, about 30 minutes. Drain well.

Fill another large bowl with cold water. Dip a rice paper wrapper very briefly into the water, then lay it on a work surface. As soon as it is soft and pliable, place a lettuce leaf in its middle. Arrange some rice noodles along the center rib of the leaf. Scatter some shrimp over the noodles and sprinkle with carrot, mint, and basil. Fold opposite ends of the wrapper over the filling. Then, starting at one side, roll up the wrapper to enclose the filling completely. With your finger, moisten the end flap to seal it shut. Transfer to a serving platter and cover with plastic wrap. Repeat with the remaining wrappers and fillings.

Serve spring rolls with hoisin and hot chili sauces for dipping.

MAKES 4 SERVINGS

Pad Thai with Shrimp

THAILAND

This version of the Thai favorite is embellished with fresh medium-sized shrimp. You could substitute ringlets of baby squid, if you wish. The briny fish sauce, widely available in Asian markets, is an essential seasoning for this dish.

½ pound narrow dried rice sticks
3 tablespoons cider vinegar
3 tablespoons sugar
¼ cup fish sauce
2 tablespoons tomato paste
3 tablespoons vegetable oil
3 medium garlic cloves, chopped fine
1 small fresh green chili, stemmed, seeded, and chopped fine
½ pound medium-sized shrimp, shelled and deveined, tails left on

2 teaspoons paprika
1 egg, lightly beaten
Romaine or butter lettuce leaves
¾ cup bean sprouts
⅓ cup toasted unsalted peanuts, chopped coarse (see Index)
1 medium scallion, cut into 1-inch shreds
¼ cup small fresh cilantro sprigs
1 small lime, cut into wedges

Put the rice sticks in a large bowl and add cold water to cover well. Leave them to soak until soft, about 30 minutes. Drain well and set aside.

Meanwhile, in a separate bowl, stir together the vinegar and sugar until the sugar dissolves. Stir in the fish sauce and tomato paste and set this seasoning mixture aside.

In a large wok or skillet, heat the oil over moderately high heat. Add the garlic and chili; as soon as they sizzle, add the shrimp and stir-fry about 30 seconds. Add the reserved seasoning mixture, sprinkle in the paprika, and then add the drained noodles; stir and turn the mixture until most of the liquid has been absorbed by the noodles. Add the egg and stir and turn the noodles gently until it sets, forming small, soft curds.

Line a serving platter with lettuce leaves and mound the noodles in the center, arranging some of the shrimp on top. Scatter the bean sprouts around the mound. Sprinkle the noodles with peanuts, scallion, and cilantro. Serve with lime wedges.

MAKES 4 SERVINGS

Rice Sticks with Seafood and Coconut Curry

MALAYSIA

You can substitute chicken if you like in this popular Malaysian curry, named *laksa* for the local spaghetti-like rice vermicelli traditionally used in it. Coconut milk, lemongrass, and briny-tasting fish sauce are all available in Asian markets and specialty food stores.

10 ounces dried thick rice vermicelli
5 cups coconut milk
4 macadamia nuts
4 medium-sized shallots, peeled and
 quartered
2 medium-sized garlic cloves, peeled
1 small fresh red or green chili, stemmed
1 tablespoon fish sauce
2 teaspoons ground coriander
1 teaspoon ground turmeric
1 teaspoon sugar
3 tablespoons vegetable oil
2 stalks fresh lemongrass, cut into 2-inch
 pieces, or 1½ tablespoons dried
 lemongrass

½ pound medium-sized shrimp, peeled
 and deveined, tails left on; or ½ pound
 firm white fish fillet, cut into ½-inch
 pieces
¼ pound fresh cooked crabmeat, flaked
 coarse
1 dozen small fresh clams, thoroughly
 rinsed and steamed until their shells
 open
Salt
White pepper
Fresh mint leaves
1 lime, cut into wedges

Put the rice noodles in a large bowl and add cold water to cover well. Leave them to soak until soft, about 30 minutes.

When the noodles are almost ready, put 1 cup of the coconut milk along with the macadamia nuts, shallots, garlic, chili, fish sauce, coriander, turmeric, and sugar in a food processor with the metal blade. Pulse several times, then process until they form a smooth paste, stopping if necessary to scrape down the bowl.

In a large wok or skillet, heat the oil over moderate heat. Add the paste and cook, stirring constantly, until the mixture gives off a rich aroma.

Stir in the lemongrass and remaining coconut milk and bring the mixture to a boil. Reduce the heat to low, add the shrimp or fish, crab, and clams, stir well, and simmer gently about 5 minutes more. Taste and adjust the seasonings with salt and white pepper.

Drain the rice noodles thoroughly and arrange in a large bowl or in four individual serving bowls. Ladle the curry over the noodles, garnish with mint leaves, and serve with lime wedges for guests to squeeze over the curry to taste.

MAKES 4 SERVINGS

Rice Sticks with Chicken, Broccoli, and Oyster Sauce

THAILAND

The Chinese influence on Thai cooking is evident in this simple stir-fried noodle dish. The bottled oyster and fish sauces—the former rich and savory, the latter bracingly briny—are both available in Asian markets and specialty food stores. Feel free to substitute beef or shrimp for the chicken. Use fresh rice sticks if available, though the recipe also will work fine with dried ones.

> ¾ pound fresh broad rice sticks or ½ pound dried broad rice sticks
> 2 tablespoons bottled oyster sauce
> 2 tablespoons light soy sauce
> 1 tablespoon fish sauce
> 2 teaspoons sugar
> ½ teaspoon white pepper
> ¼ cup vegetable oil
> 2 medium-sized garlic cloves, chopped fine
> 3 cups small broccoli florets
> ¾ pound boneless skinless chicken breast, cut crosswise into ¼-inch-thick slices

If using fresh rice noodles, put them in a colander or strainer. Bring a pot or kettle of water to a boil and pour over the noodles to rinse, soften, and warm them. If using dried rice noodles, put them in a large bowl and add cold water to cover well. Leave them to soak until soft, about 30 minutes. Drain the noodles thoroughly.

In a small bowl, stir together the oyster, soy, and fish sauces with the sugar and pepper. Set aside.

In a large wok or skillet, heat 1 tablespoon of the oil over moderately high heat. Add the garlic; as soon as it sizzles, add the broccoli and stir-fry until bright green, about 2 minutes; remove and set aside.

Add 1 more tablespoon of the oil to the wok. Add the chicken and stir-fry until just cooked through, 2 to 3 minutes. Remove and set aside.

Add the remaining oil to the wok, add the noodles, and gently stir-fry until their edges begin to brown, 2 to 3 minutes. Add the reserved broccoli, chicken, and sauce mixture and stir-fry 1 minute more, until all the ingredients are heated through and evenly coated.

MAKES 4 SERVINGS

Rice Sticks with Chicken, Tomatoes, and Curry

THAILAND

❧

Hints of curry and sugar give this mild noodle dish a pleasantly spicy-sweet flavor. Though it can be made with dried rice sticks, it is more authentic made with fresh rice stick noodles purchased from an Asian market—where you'll also find the briny-tasting fish sauce. Many supermarkets now sell already ground chicken; if not, buy boneless, skinless breasts and chop them in a food processor with the metal blade.

¾ pound fresh broad rice sticks or ½ pound dried broad rice sticks
3 tablespoons light soy sauce
1 tablespoon fish sauce
1 tablespoon brown sugar
1 tablespoon curry powder
¼ cup vegetable oil
2 medium-sized garlic cloves, chopped fine

¾ pound ground chicken
4 medium-sized, firm, ripe tomatoes, cored, quartered, stemmed, seeded, and cut into ¼-inch-wide slices
2 tablespoons coarsely chopped fresh cilantro leaves

If using fresh rice noodles, put them in a colander or strainer. Bring a pot or kettle of water to a boil and pour over the noodles to rinse, soften, and warm them. If using dried rice noodles, put them in a large bowl and add cold water to cover well. Leave them to soak until soft, about 30 minutes. Drain the noodles thoroughly.

In a small bowl, stir together the soy and fish sauces with the sugar and curry powder. Set aside.

In a large wok or skillet, heat 2 tablespoons of the oil over moderately high heat. Add the garlic; as soon as it sizzles, add the chicken and stir-fry, breaking it up into small pieces, until it loses its pink color, 2 to 3 minutes; remove and set aside.

Add the remaining oil to the wok, add the noodles, and gently stir-fry until their edges begin to brown, 2 to 3 minutes. Add the reserved chicken, tomatoes, and the reserved sauce mixture and stir-fry 1 minute more, until all the ingredients are heated through and evenly coated. Garnish with cilantro.

· MAKES 4 SERVINGS

Rice Sticks with Beef and Spinach

CHINA

A quick and colorful stir-fry tops lightly fried rice noodles in this Chinese-inspired dish, seasoned with the Chinese sauce of fermented black soybeans widely available in Asian markets and specialty food stores.

½ pound narrow dried rice sticks
3 tablespoons light soy sauce
2 tablespoons cornstarch
2 teaspoons dry sherry
½ teaspoon white pepper
½ pound lean beef steak, trimmed and cut into ¼-inch-thick slices
¼ cup vegetable oil
2 medium-sized garlic cloves, chopped fine

¾ pound small spinach leaves, stemmed, thoroughly washed and dried
¾ cup chicken broth
1 tablespoon bottled Chinese black-bean sauce
1 tablespoon toasted sesame seeds (see Index)

—123—

Put the rice sticks in a large bowl and add cold water to cover well. Leave them to soak until soft, about 30 minutes. Drain well.

Meanwhile, in another bowl, stir 1 tablespoon each of the soy sauce and cornstarch together with the sherry and pepper. Add the beef, stir well, and marinate at room temperature about 15 minutes. In a smaller bowl or cup, stir together the remaining soy sauce and cornstarch and set aside.

In a large wok or skillet, heat half of the oil over moderately high heat. Add the drained noodles and stir-fry for 1 minute. Transfer to a heated platter and set aside.

Add the remaining oil and the garlic to the wok; as soon as the garlic sizzles, add the beef and stir-fry until it is no longer pink, 1 to 2 minutes. Add the spinach, broth, black-bean sauce, and reserved soy-cornstarch mixture. Continue stirring until the sauce thickens to coating consistency, 2 to 3 minutes more. Spoon over the reserved noodles and garnish with sesame seeds.

MAKES 4 SERVINGS

Classic Pad Thai

Pork, shrimp, and chicken combine to make this the most elaborate of all the versions of the popular Thai street vendor's dish. The briny fish sauce—sold in Asian markets—is an essential seasoning. Tomato paste enhances the color and flavor.

½ pound narrow dried rice sticks

3 tablespoons lime juice

2 tablespoons sugar

3 tablespoons fish sauce

2 tablespoons tomato paste

½ pound pork tenderloin, cut crosswise into ¼-inch-thick slices

½ pound boneless skinless chicken breast, cut crosswise into ¼-inch-thick slices

¼ cup vegetable oil

2 medium-sized shallots, chopped fine

1 medium-sized garlic clove, chopped fine

1 fresh green chili, stemmed, seeded, and chopped fine

¼ pound medium-sized shrimp, shelled and deveined, tails left on

2 teaspoons paprika

2 eggs, lightly beaten

Romaine or butter lettuce leaves

1 cup bean sprouts

⅓ cup toasted unsalted peanuts, chopped coarse (see Index)

2 medium-sized scallions, cut into 1-inch shreds

¼ cup shredded fresh basil leaves

1 small lime, cut into wedges

Put the rice sticks in a large bowl and add cold water to cover well. Leave them to soak until soft, about 30 minutes. At the same time, in a separate bowl, stir together the lime juice and sugar until the sugar dissolves. Stir in the fish sauce and tomato paste, add the pork and chicken, toss well, and set aside to marinate at room temperature.

Drain the noodles well and set aside.

In a large wok or skillet, heat the oil over moderately high heat. Add the shallots, garlic, and chili; as soon as they sizzle, add the reserved pork, chicken, and seasoning mixture and stir-fry about 1 minute. Add the shrimp and stir-fry 30 seconds more. Sprinkle in the paprika and then add the reserved drained noodles; stir and turn until most of the liquid has been absorbed by the noodles. Add the eggs and stir and turn the noodles gently until they set, forming small, soft curds.

Line a serving bowl or platter with the lettuce leaves and mound the noodles in the center, arranging some of the shrimp on top. Scatter the bean sprouts around the mound. Sprinkle the noodles with peanuts, scallions, and basil. Arrange lime wedges around the sides, to be squeezed over individual portions.

MAKES 4 SERVINGS

Mee Krob

THAILAND

Traditionally served at special celebrations, this noodle dish rightly deserves popularity for its beguiling combination of crisp noodles coated in a sticky sauce balancing sweet, (brown sugar), salty (soy sauce and briny Asian fish sauce), and sour (vinegar) flavors.

Vegetable oil for deep frying
6 ounces thin rice vermicelli
¼ cup brown sugar
¼ cup cider vinegar
3 tablespoons fish sauce
1 tablespoon light soy sauce
3 garlic cloves, chopped fine
2 small red or green fresh chilies, halved
  lengthwise, stemmed, seeded, and
  chopped fine
1 medium-sized shallot, chopped fine
¼ pound pork tenderloin, cut crosswise
  into ⅛-inch-thick slices
¼ pound medium-sized shrimp, shelled
  and deveined, tails left on
1 medium-sized red bell pepper,
  quartered, stemmed, seeded, each
  quarter cut crosswise into ¼-inch slices
2 cups bean sprouts
1 medium-sized scallion, sliced thin
¼ cup finely chopped fresh cilantro
  leaves
1 lime, cut into wedges

Preheat the oven to 200°F.
In a large wok or heavy skillet, heat several inches of oil to 350°F on a deep-frying

thermometer. Drop about ⅙ of the noodles into the oil; using a wire skimmer or slotted spoon to turn them and keep them immersed, fry until they puff up uniformly, about 15 seconds. Remove to drain on paper towels, then transfer to a baking pan and keep warm in the oven. Repeat with the remaining batches of noodles.

In a mixing bowl, stir together the sugar, vinegar, fish and soy sauces. Set this sauce mixture aside.

Carefully pour off all but a few tablespoons of the oil from the wok or skillet. Over moderately high heat, add the garlic, chilies, and shallot. As soon as they sizzle, add the pork and stir-fry until it loses its pink color, 1 to 2 minutes; add the shrimp and stir-fry until they turn pink, about 30 seconds more. Add the reserved sauce mixture and stir until it is thick, bubbly, and smooth, 2 to 3 minutes.

Remove the wok or skillet from the heat and continue stirring about 1 minute more. Add the crisp noodles and bell pepper. Using two long-handled spoons or fork, turn the noodles in the sauce to coat them evenly and distribute the pork, shrimp, and bell pepper among the noodles.

Mound the noodle mixture on top of a serving platter and surround with bean sprouts. Top with scallion and cilantro and serve with lime wedges to be squeezed over individual portions.

MAKES 4 SERVINGS

Griddled Marinated Beef with Rice Sticks

VIETNAM

The mild flavor and texture of fine rice noodles provide a perfect foil for marinated, crisply cooked pieces of beef in this simple yet elegant preparation. If you like, substitute pork tenderloin for the beef, or replace half the meat with medium-sized fresh shrimp. The marinade beguilingly combines the sweetness of sugar with the tang of lime juice and the brininess of fish sauce—the latter condiment readily available at Asian markets along with the sweet-savory hoisin and pungent chili sauces.

1 tablespoon fish sauce
1 tablespoon lime juice
1 tablespoon sugar
2 tablespoons vegetable oil
2 medium-sized garlic cloves, chopped
   fine
1 pound lean beef steak, trimmed and
   cut crosswise into ⅛-inch-thick slices
3 ounces thin rice vermicelli
12 small butter lettuce leaves, stem ends
   cut out
2 medium-sized cucumbers, peeled and
   shredded coarse
1 medium-sized carrot, peeled and
   shredded coarse
⅓ cup packed whole fresh mint leaves
⅓ cup packed whole fresh basil leaves
⅓ cup packed whole fresh cilantro leaves
12 dried rice paper wrappers
Hoisin sauce
Hot chili sauce
2 limes, cut into wedges

In a mixing bowl, stir together the fish sauce, lime juice, sugar, vegetable oil, and garlic. Add the beef, toss well to coat, and leave to marinate at room temperature while you soak the noodles.

Put the rice noodles in a large bowl and add cold water to cover well. Leave them to soak until soft, about 30 minutes. Drain well.

Arrange the noodles on a serving platter, separating any large clumps with your fingers. On the same platter or another platter, arrange the lettuce, cucumbers, carrot, mint, basil, and cilantro. Arrange the rice paper wrappers on a separate plate, and fill a large bowl with cold water. Place the platters, plate, and bowl in the center of the dining table.

Preheat a large, heavy skillet or griddle over high heat. Without crowding, arrange slices of beef in a single layer on the skillet and cook until evenly seared, 1 to 2 minutes per side; transfer to a heated platter and repeat with remaining meat.

To serve, place the beef on the table with the other ingredients. Let the guests quickly dip rice paper wrappers in the water and transfer them to their individual dining plates; when soft and pliable, the wrappers are individually topped with lettuce, then noodles, beef, cucumbers, carrot, and herbs, before being folded and rolled up to be dipped in a mixture of hoisin and chili sauce blended to taste with squeezes of lime.

MAKES 4 SERVINGS

Singapore Noodles with Pork

SINGAPORE

Typical of the food served by Chinese street vendors in Singapore marketplaces. Substitute beef or chicken for the pork, if you like.

10 ounces thin rice vermicelli
¼ cup light soy sauce
2 teaspoons hot chili oil
2 teaspoons brown sugar
2 teaspoons grated fresh gingerroot
½ teaspoon ground black pepper
1 pound pork tenderloin, cut crosswise into ¼-inch-thick slices
3 tablespoons vegetable oil

2 medium-sized garlic cloves, chopped fine
2 medium-sized scallions, cut into 1-inch shreds
1 medium-sized onion, sliced thin
1 cup coarsely shredded carrots
2 tablespoons finely chopped fresh cilantro leaves

Put the rice noodles in a large bowl and add cold water to cover well. Leave them to soak until soft, about 30 minutes. Drain well and set aside.

Meanwhile, stir together the soy sauce, chili oil, sugar, ginger, and black pepper. Transfer about a third of the mixture to another bowl and toss it with the pork, leaving it to marinate at room temperature while the noodles soak; reserve the remaining two-thirds.

In a large wok or skillet, heat the oil over moderately high heat. Add the garlic, scallions, and onion; as soon as they sizzle, add the pork and stir-fry until it loses its pink color, about 2 minutes. Add the drained noodles and the carrots and stir-fry about 1 minute more.

Add the reserved soy sauce mixture and stir-fry until most of the liquid has been absorbed, about 1 minute more. Transfer to a platter and garnish with cilantro.

MAKES 4 SERVINGS

6
Couscous

Couscous is the almost forgotten stepchild of the noodle world. Although it looks like a grain and often is considered as such, it is, in fact, North Africa's answer to pasta and therefore a close cousin of the world's many and varied noodles: small pellets of a semolina-and-water dough that have a subtle flavor and a pleasantly granular texture ideal for sopping up savory juices.

Traditional couscous, as you would find it in its native lands, requires a somewhat involved preparation that long prevented it from achieving the popularity that it deserves elsewhere. Before cooking, the small granules were sprinkled with cold water, left to soak for half an hour, and then fluffed to separate them; only then were they steamed for 30 minutes more above the stew they would accompany, usually in a special two-tiered cooking apparatus called a *couscoussier.*

Rather than go through such an involved process, I've taken advantage of the quick-cooking form of couscous now widely available in food markets and ethnic delis. (I use a boxed product labeled "Couscous Moroccan Pasta" from Near East Food Products Co., Leominster, MA 01453.) These granules, already precooked and then dried, require only a brief 5-minute steeping in hot liquid to yield ready-to-eat couscous with outstanding flavor and texture.

Couscous Salad with Chicken, Spring Vegetables, and Mint Vinaigrette

UNITED STATES

Just like pasta or rice, couscous provides an excellent foundation for a Western-style main-course luncheon or a buffet salad. This recipe makes smart use of leftover chicken, although you certainly can cook some expressly for the salad if you like. Feel free to substitute cooked turkey, or even canned tuna.

2¼ cups water or chicken broth

1 teaspoon salt

8 ounces quick-cooking couscous

2 cups coarsely chopped cooked chicken meat

1 cup shelled fresh or frozen peas, cooked in boiling water until tender-crisp

2 medium-sized carrots, cut into ½-inch cubes and cooked in boiling water until tender-crisp

2 medium-sized zucchini, cut into ½-inch cubes and cooked in boiling water until tender-crisp

2 medium-sized Roma tomatoes, cored, halved, stemmed, seeded, and cut into ½-inch pieces

¼ cup finely chopped fresh parsley

¼ cup finely chopped fresh chives

¼ cup fresh lemon juice

1 tablespoon finely chopped fresh mint leaves

¼ teaspoon sugar

¼ teaspoon white pepper

¾ cup extra-virgin olive oil

1 head red leaf, romaine, or butter lettuce, leaves separated

Fresh mint or parsley sprigs

In a medium-sized saucepan, bring the water or broth to a boil with ½ teaspoon of salt. Sprinkle and stir in the couscous; cover the pan and remove it from the heat. After 5 minutes, uncover the couscous and fluff it lightly with a fork.

Transfer the couscous to a mixing bowl and toss it well with the chicken, peas, carrots, zucchini, tomatoes, parsley, and chives.

In a small bowl, stir together the lemon juice, mint, remaining ½ teaspoon salt, sugar, and pepper. When the salt and sugar have dissolved, stir in the olive oil. Pour the dressing over the couscous mixture and toss well. Taste and adjust the seasonings. Cover with plastic wrap and refrigerate for 1 to 3 hours before serving.

Arrange the lettuce leaves on a serving platter and mound the couscous mixture in the middle. Garnish with mint or parsley sprigs.

MAKES 4 SERVINGS

Couscous with Spiced Vegetable Stew

MOROCCO

Serve as a vegetarian main course or as a side dish to grilled or roast meat or chicken.

¼ cup olive oil
4 tablespoons unsalted butter
2 medium-sized garlic cloves, chopped fine
1 medium-sized onion, chopped fine
1 tablespoon grated fresh gingerroot
1 small fresh green or red chili pepper,
    halved, stemmed, seeded, and finely
    chopped
2 teaspoons crushed red chili flakes
1 28-ounce can whole tomatoes
2 medium-sized carrots, cut into 1½-inch
    chunks
2 medium-sized parsnips, cut into 1½-
    inch chunks
2 medium-sized zucchini, cut into 1½-
    inch chunks
1 medium-sized eggplant, cut into 1½-
    inch chunks
1 medium-sized green bell pepper,
    halved, stemmed, seeded, and cut into
    1½-inch squares
½ pound string beans, cut into 1½-inch pieces
2 tablespoons tomato paste
1 tablespoon sugar
3 cups water or chicken broth
10 ounces quick-cooking couscous
¾ cup seedless brown or golden raisins
¼ cup coarsely chopped fresh cilantro

In a medium-sized skillet or saucepan, heat the oil with 2 tablespoons of the butter over moderate heat. Add the garlic, onion, and ginger; sauté until tender, 2 to 3 minutes. Add the chili pepper and chili flakes and sauté 1 minute more. Add the tomatoes, breaking them up with your hands. Stir in the carrots, parsnips, zucchini, eggplant, bell pepper, beans, tomato paste, and sugar.

Raise the heat slightly and simmer the sauce, stirring frequently, until the vegetables are just tender and the liquid has reduced to a coating consistency, about 15 minutes.

About halfway through the simmering of the vegetable stew, bring the water or broth to a boil with the remaining butter in a medium-sized saucepan. Sprinkle and stir in the couscous and raisins; cover the pan and remove it from the heat.

As soon as the vegetables are done and the couscous has sat for about 5 minutes, uncover the couscous and fluff it lightly with a fork. Mound the couscous in a wide serving bowl or on a platter with a raised rim. Make a well in the center of the couscous and spoon the vegetable stew into the well. Garnish with cilantro.

—135—

MAKES 4 SERVINGS

Couscous "Taboulleh"

UNITED STATES

Having a texture and size similar to cracked bulgur wheat, couscous makes an intriguing, subtle substitute for that robust grain in this new American take on a traditional Middle Eastern salad. Serve it as a summer luncheon course or buffet offering, or as an accompaniment to grilled poultry, meat, or seafood.

1½ cups water
Salt
5 ounces quick-cooking couscous
¾ cup finely chopped fresh parsley
½ cup finely chopped fresh mint
½ cup thinly sliced scallions
3 large, firm, ripe Roma tomatoes, cored, seeded, and chopped fine
½ small red onion, chopped fine

¼ cup lemon juice
1 medium-sized garlic clove, pressed through a garlic press
⅓ cup extra-virgin olive oil
White pepper
1 head butter lettuce, leaves separated
Fresh mint or parsley sprigs, for garnish
1 lemon, cut into wedges

In a medium-sized saucepan, bring the water to a boil with ½ teaspoon of salt. Sprinkle and stir in the couscous; cover the pan and remove it from the heat. After 5 minutes, uncover the couscous and fluff it lightly with a fork.

Transfer the couscous to a mixing bowl and toss it well with the parsley, mint, scallions, tomatoes, and onion.

In a small bowl, stir together the lemon juice, ½ teaspoon more salt, and the garlic. When the salt has dissolved, stir in the olive oil. Pour the dressing over the couscous mixture and toss well. Taste and adjust the seasonings with salt and white pepper. Cover with plastic wrap and refrigerate for 1 to 3 hours before serving.

Arrange the lettuce leaves on a serving platter and mound the couscous mixture in the middle. Garnish with mint or parsley sprigs and lemon wedges.

MAKES 4 SERVINGS

Couscous with Cumin-Dusted Salmon, Bell Peppers, and Pine Nuts

UNITED STATES

Quick-cooking couscous makes an ideal accompaniment for seared salmon fillets exotically spiced with cumin.

3 cups seafood broth or water	¼ cup olive oil
10 ounces quick-cooking couscous	4 medium-sized red or yellow bell
2 tablespoons all-purpose flour	peppers, roasted, peeled, seeded (see
1 tablespoon ground cumin	Index), and torn into ¼-inch-wide
4 thin fresh salmon fillets, about 6	strips, juices reserved
ounces each	2 tablespoons finely chopped parsley
Salt	1 tablespoon lemon juice
White pepper	¼ cup pine nuts, toasted (see Index)

Bring the broth or water to a boil in a medium-sized saucepan. Sprinkle and stir in the couscous; cover the pan and remove it from the heat.

Meanwhile, in a small bowl, stir together the flour and cumin. Season the salmon fillets evenly with salt and pepper and dust lightly on both sides with the flour-cumin mixture.

In a large skillet, heat the oil over moderate to high heat. Add the salmon and sauté until just cooked through, 2 to 3 minutes per side. Remove from the skillet and keep warm.

Add the peppers and their juices, the parsley, and lemon juice to the pan and sauté just until heated, about 1 minute.

Fluff the couscous lightly with a fork. Mound it on four individual serving plates. Make a well in the center and spoon the pepper mixture into it. Top with the salmon fillets and garnish with pine nuts.

MAKES 4 SERVINGS

Couscous with Chicken, Carrots, Saffron, and Raisins

MOROCCO

Perfumed with saffron, this simple chicken stew shines with a golden color against a bed of parsley-flecked couscous.

¼ cup olive oil
4 tablespoons unsalted butter
¾ cup all-purpose flour
1 whole (3½ pound) broiler/fryer chicken, cut into 8 pieces, or equivalent weight of already cut-up pieces
Salt
2 medium-sized garlic cloves, chopped fine
1 medium-sized onion, chopped fine
1½ quarts chicken broth
1 cup seedless golden or brown raisins
¾ teaspoon powdered saffron or saffron threads
3 medium-sized carrots, cut into ½-inch-thick slices
10 ounces quick-cooking couscous
Black pepper
¾ cup coarsely chopped fresh parsley
Fresh parsley sprigs

In a large skillet, heat the oil and half of the butter over moderate heat. Sprinkle the flour evenly onto a dinner plate. When the butter begins to sizzle, sprinkle the chicken pieces with salt, roll them in the flour until evenly coated, and add them to the skillet. Sauté until golden brown, 3 to 4 minutes per side. Remove the chicken from the skillet.

Pour off all but about 2 tablespoons of the oil-butter mixture. Add the garlic and onion and sauté until translucent, 2 to 3 minutes. Add 2½ cups of the broth, raise the heat, and stir and scrape with a wooden spoon to dissolve the pan deposits. Reduce the heat to low, add the chicken pieces, and scatter in the raisins.

Dissolve the saffron in another ½ cup of the broth and pour it into the skillet. Cover and simmer gently until the chicken is tender, 30 to 40 minutes. About halfway through the simmering, add the carrots.

When the chicken is done, bring the remaining broth to a boil with the remaining butter in a medium-sized saucepan. Sprinkle and stir in the couscous; cover the pan and remove it from the heat. Leave to sit for about 5 minutes.

Meanwhile, uncover the chicken and, if its cooking liquid is a bit thin, raise the heat and simmer briskly to reduce it to a coating consistency. Taste and adjust the seasonings with salt and pepper.

Add the chopped parsley to the couscous and fluff them together lightly with a fork. Mound the couscous in a wide serving bowl, on a platter with a raised rim, or on four individual serving bowls or plates. Make a well in the center and spoon the chicken stew into the well. Garnish with parsley sprigs.

MAKES 4 SERVINGS

Cinnamon-Scented Couscous with Beef Stew and Prunes

UNITED STATES

Rich, heady flavors predominate here, with a robust stew complemented by an aromatic couscous. Try this recipe with pork, if you like.

2 tablespoons vegetable oil
1½ pounds boneless beef stewing meat,
    cut into 1-inch pieces
Salt and black pepper
1 tablespoon unsalted butter
1 medium-sized onion, chopped fine
⅛ teaspoon allspice
⅛ teaspoon ground cloves
⅛ teaspoon ground ginger
⅛ teaspoon grated nutmeg
5 cups beef broth
1 cup dark beer
1 cup small pitted prunes
2 medium-sized carrots, cut into ½-inch
    pieces
2 tablespoons unsalted butter
1 (3- to 4-inch) cinnamon stick
10 ounces quick-cooking couscous
¼ cup slivered almonds, toasted (see
    Index)
2 tablespoons coarsely chopped fresh
    parsley

In a large saucepan or skillet, heat the oil over moderate heat. Season the beef pieces with salt and pepper and add just enough to the pan to fit without overcrowding;

sauté until evenly browned, 3 to 5 minutes, and remove from the pan. Repeat with the remaining beef.

Pour off all but about a tablespoon of the fat from the pan. Add 1 tablespoon butter and as soon as it has melted, sauté the onion until it begins to brown, 3 to 5 minutes. Add the allspice, cloves, ginger, and nutmeg and sauté 1 minute more. Add 2 cups of the broth along with the beer, raise the heat, and bring to a boil. Reduce the heat to low, add the prunes and carrots, cover, and simmer very gently until the beef is tender, 1 to 1½ hours, adding a little more broth if necessary to keep the stew moist.

When the beef is tender, put the remaining broth, the remaining butter, and the cinnamon stick in a medium-sized saucepan and bring to a boil. Sprinkle and stir in the couscous; cover the pan and remove it from the heat. After 5 minutes, uncover the couscous and fluff it lightly with a fork, removing the cinnamon. Mound the couscous in a wide serving bowl, on a platter with a raised rim, or on four individual serving bowls or plates.

Taste the beef stew and adjust the seasonings to taste. Make a well in the center of the couscous and spoon the stew into the well. Garnish with almonds and parsley.

MAKES 4 SERVINGS

Couscous with Sweet-and-Sour Braised Veal Shanks and Chick-Peas

TUNISIA

This variation on Milanese osso buco takes an exotic North African turn with its combination of fresh fruit juices and the addition of chick-peas, making couscous as natural an accompaniment as the traditional Italian cornmeal polenta. A good butcher will cut slices of bone-in veal shank to order.

2 tablespoons olive oil
½ cup all-purpose flour
8 (1½-inch-thick) slices veal shank
Salt and white pepper
2 medium-sized garlic cloves, chopped
    fine
1 medium-sized onion, chopped fine
1 medium-sized carrot, chopped fine
1 16-ounce can whole tomatoes
3 cups chicken broth
3 cups orange juice
2 cups drained canned chick-peas
¼ cup lemon juice
1 tablespoon dried basil
10 ounces quick-cooking couscous
2 tablespoons finely chopped fresh
    parsley
2 tablespoons grated lemon zest

In a skillet large enough to hold the veal comfortably in a single layer, heat the olive oil over moderate heat. Meanwhile, spread the flour on a dinner plate. Sprinkle the veal slices with salt and pepper and turn them in the flour until evenly coated. Add the veal to the skillet and sauté until evenly browned, 3 to 4 minutes per side. Remove from the skillet and set aside.

Add the garlic, onion, and carrot and sauté until lightly browned, 3 to 4 minutes. Return the reserved veal to the skillet and add the tomatoes, crushing them with your fingers. Add half each of the broth and orange juice. Add the chick-peas, lemon juice, and basil. Bring to a boil; reduce the heat and simmer, covered, until the veal is very tender, about 1½ hours.

When the veal is done, bring the remaining broth and orange juice to a boil in a medium-sized saucepan. Sprinkle and stir in the couscous; cover the pan and remove it from the heat. Leave to sit for about 5 minutes.

Meanwhile, uncover the veal and, if its cooking liquid is a bit thin, raise the heat and simmer briskly to reduce it to a coating consistency. Taste and adjust the seasonings.

Fluff the couscous lightly with a fork. Mound it in a wide serving bowl, on a platter with a raised rim, or on four individual serving bowls or plates. Make a well in the center and transfer the veal and its sauce into the well. Garnish with parsley and lemon zest.

MAKES 4 SERVINGS

Couscous with Lamb and Apricots

ALGERIA

Couscous's mild flavor and grain-like texture complement the savory, sweet, and tart tastes of a simple stew of lamb and dried apricots.

2 tablespoons vegetable oil
1½ pounds boneless lamb stewing meat,
    cut into 1-inch pieces
Salt and black pepper
1 tablespoon unsalted butter
1 medium-sized onion, chopped fine
1 teaspoon cumin
1 teaspoon hot paprika
¼ teaspoon cinnamon
1½ quarts beef broth or chicken broth
1 cup dried apricots, cut into ¼- to ½-
    inch pieces
10 ounces quick-cooking couscous
¼ cup slivered almonds, toasted (see
    Index)
2 tablespoons finely chopped fresh mint
    leaves

In a large saucepan or skillet, heat the oil over moderate heat. Season the lamb pieces with salt and pepper and add just enough to the pan to fit without overcrowding; sauté until evenly browned, 3 to 5 minutes, and remove from the pan. Repeat with the remaining lamb.

Pour off all but about a tablespoon of fat from the pan. Add the butter and, as soon as it has melted, sauté the onion until it begins to brown, 3 to 5 minutes. Add the cumin, paprika, and cinnamon and sauté 1 minute more. Add half of the broth, raise the heat, and bring to a boil. Reduce the heat to low, add the apricots, cover, and simmer very gently until the lamb is tender, 1 to 1½ hours, adding a little more broth if necessary to keep the stew moist.

When the lamb is tender, bring the remaining broth to a boil in a medium-sized saucepan. Sprinkle and stir in the couscous; cover the pan and remove it from the heat. After 5 minutes, uncover the couscous and fluff it lightly with a fork. Mound the couscous in a wide serving bowl, on a platter with a raised rim, or on four individual serving bowls or plates.

Taste the lamb stew and adjust the seasonings to taste. Make a well in the center of the couscous and spoon the stew into the well. Garnish with almonds and mint.

MAKES 4 SERVINGS

Breakfast Couscous with Dates and Almonds

MOROCCO

The mild-yet-distinctive flavor of couscous, and the speed with which the quick-cooking variety is prepared, makes it an ideal breakfast cereal.

3 cups milk
4 tablespoons unsalted butter
10 ounces quick-cooking couscous
½ cup finely chopped pitted dates
½ cup slivered almonds, toasted (see Index)
Honey
Half-and-half or cream (optional)

In a medium-sized saucepan, bring the milk and butter to a boil. Sprinkle and stir in the couscous; cover the pan, remove it from the heat, and let it sit for about 5 minutes.

Uncover the pan, add the dates and almonds, and use a fork to fluff them together with the couscous. Spoon the couscous into four individual serving bowls and let each guest drizzle to taste with honey and, if desired, add a little half-and-half or cream.

MAKES 4 SERVINGS

Couscous Pudding with Raisins, Orange, and Cardamom

MOROCCO

Ground cardamom adds a delicate perfume to a simple dessert pudding that provides all the satisfaction of more familiar rice puddings. If you like, buy some extra cream to whip as a garnish for the pudding.

3 cups milk
½ cup unsalted butter, softened
10 ounces quick-cooking couscous
1 cup whipping cream
⅓ cup orange marmalade
4 eggs, lightly beaten
½ cup seedless golden or brown raisins
¼ cup honey, at room temperature
¼ teaspoon ground cardamom

Preheat the oven to 350°F.

In a large saucepan, bring the milk and half of the butter to a boil. Sprinkle and stir in the couscous; cover the pan, remove it from the heat, and let it stand 5 minutes.

Transfer the couscous to a mixing bowl. In a separate bowl or measuring cup, use a fork to stir together the cream and marmalade, breaking up and dissolving the marmalade with the fork. Stir the mixture into the couscous, then stir in the eggs, raisins, honey, and cardamom.

With the remaining butter, generously grease the inside of a 2-quart baking dish. Bake in the preheated oven until golden brown, 30 to 40 minutes. Serve hot or cold.

MAKES 4 SERVINGS

INDEX

—149—

About the Author

Norman Kolpas is the bestselling author of more than two dozen cookbooks, including the highly acclaimed *Pasta Presto, Whole-Meal Salads*, and *Pizza California Style*. As a leading magazine and book editor, he has worked closely with such renowned culinary experts as Richard Olney, Jeremiah Tower, Jacques Pepin, and Elisabeth Lambert Ortiz. In addition, he teaches a popular class at UCLA on writing and publishing cookbooks.

Mr. Kolpas lives in Los Angeles. He and his wife, writer Katie Goldman, have one son, Jacob.